BRIDGING GRADES 2 to 3

Summer Bridge®
An imprint of Carson Dellosa Education
PO Box 35665
Greensboro, NC 27425 USA

© 2025 Carson Dellosa Education. Except as permitted under the United States Copyright Act, no part of this publication may be reproduced, stored, or distributed in any form or by any means (mechanically, electronically, recording, etc.) without the prior written consent of Carson Dellosa Education. Summer Bridge® is an imprint of Carson Dellosa Education.

Printed in the USA • All rights reserved.
ISBN 978-1-4838-7271-1
2-062251151

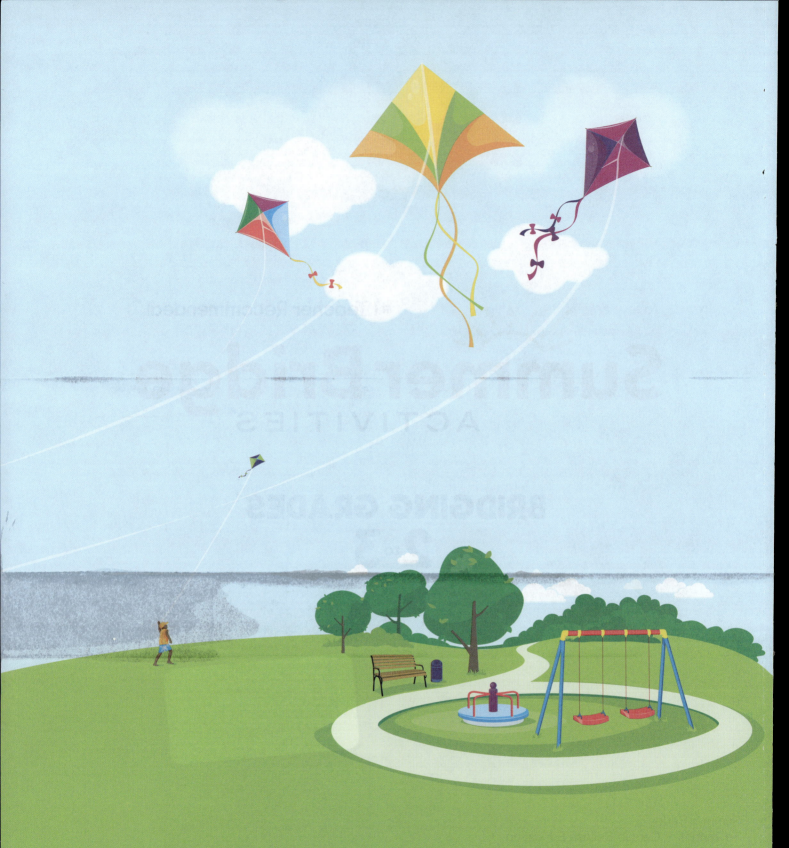

Caution: Exercise activities may require adult supervision. Before beginning any exercise activity, consult a physician. Written parental permission is suggested for those using this book in group situations. Children should always warm up prior to beginning any exercise activity and should stop immediately if they feel any discomfort during exercise.

Caution: Before completing any balloon activity, ask parents' permission and inquire about possible latex allergies. Also, remember that uninflated or popped balloons may present a choking hazard.

The authors and publisher are not responsible or liable for any injury that may result from performing the exercises or activities in this book.

Table of Contents

How to Use Your *Summer Bridge Activities* Book 4
Skills Matrix 6
Summer Reading Ideas 8
Summer Reading BINGO 9
Section 1: Monthly Goals and Word List 10
Introduction to Flexibility 11
Let's Play Today Activities 12
Activity Pages 13
Science Experiments 53
Social Studies Activities 55
Section 2: Monthly Goals and Word List 58
Introduction to Strength 59
Let's Play Today Activities 60
Activity Pages 61
Science Experiments 101
Social Studies Activities 103
Section 3: Monthly Goals and Word List 106
Introduction to Endurance 107
Let's Play Today Activities 108
Activity Pages 109
Science Experiments 149
Social Studies Activities 151
Reflect and Reset 154
Answer Key 156
Flash Cards
Manipulatives
Progress Chart
Reference Chart

How To Use Your *Summer Bridge Activities*® Book

Three Summer Months, 15 Minutes a Day

The three color-coded sections match the three months of summer. Your child has two pages to complete each weekday (a front and a back), taking about 15 minutes total. The activities are designed to reinforce second-grade skills and introduce third-grade topics.

Special Features

Summer Reading Fun:

free e-books, summer reading log, and ideas to make reading fun

Charts and Poster:

a helpful fact reference chart, a progress chart with stickers, and a summer bucket list poster

Science and Social Studies Activities:

monthly hands-on science experiments and interesting social studies activities

Flash Cards:

tear-out flash cards for hands-on practice

Healthy Habits Sidebars

Mindful Moments

activities focused on social and emotional learning

Let's Play Today

activities encouraging physical activity and play

Fast Fun Facts

fun trivia facts that inspire a love of learning

© Carson Dellosa Education

The adventure continues online with IXL!

Throughout this edition of Summer Bridge Activities®, you'll see 3-digit codes that connect your family with fun, motivating online practice questions on IXL, the most widely used K-12 online learning program in the U.S. On IXL.com or the IXL mobile app, simply type the 3-digit code into the Skill ID box to start "playing" IXL and earning fun awards and certificates!

Try IXL free with 10 questions per day, and learn about how an IXL membership can boost learning even further. With an IXL account you'll get:

Limitless learning
Boost learning and curiosity with over 17,000 topics in math, English, science, social studies, and Spanish for everyone, from K-12.

Support and encouragement
Get instant feedback, step-by-step explanations, videos, and more! IXL makes it easy to learn from mistakes and feel good about it.

Awards and certificates
Whimsical awards and certificates celebrate your child's achievements and keep them motivated.

A unique plan for every child
IXL builds a growth path for your child by meeting them at their learning level and giving them exactly what they need to work on next.

The learning app families trust
In over 75 scientific research studies, IXL is proven to help students make bigger learning gains and build confidence in their abilities. No wonder it's used by 1 in 4 students across the U.S.!

Ready to open up an exciting new world of learning?

Join hundreds of thousands of parents across the world and give your child access to unlimited learning with an IXL membership!

Learn more at
ixl.com/summer-bridge/2-3

Skills Matrix

Day	Addition	Algebra	Division	Fractions	Geometry & Measurement	Grammar	Graphing & Probability	Language Arts	Multiplication	Number Sense	Phonics	Problem Solving	Reading Comprehension	Science	Social Studies	Subtraction	Time & Money	Vocabulary & Spelling	Writing
1					★			★		★									
2		★								★							★		
3				★						★		★							
4	★									★	★								
5	★			★						★									
6						★				★			★						
7						★	★												★
8						★	★				★							★	
9	★					★				★						★		★	
10	★															★		★	
11										★	★							★	
12	★					★		★										★	
13						★	★						★						
14	★					★										★			★
15								★			★							★	
16					★						★	★							
17	★					★				★						★			
18	★															★	★	★	
19										★			★	★					
20	★					★		★										★	★
Bonus			★		★		★				★	★	★					★	★
1	★					★		★									★		
2						★							★			★			
3	★					★			★							★			
4				★	★	★		★											★
5	★					★							★			★			★
6																	★	★	
7					★												★	★	
8						★							★			★			
9						★			★								★		
10						★	★		★								★		

© Carson Dellosa Education

Skills Matrix

Day	Addition	Algebra	Division	Fractions	Geometry & Measurement	Grammar	Graphing & Probability	Language Arts	Multiplication	Number Sense	Phonics	Problem Solving	Reading Comprehension	Science	Social Studies	Subtraction	Time & Money	Vocabulary & Spelling	Writing
11						★							★				★		
12						★				★			★				★		★
13						★						★	★						
14					★								★					★	
15					★	★							★						★
16					★			★										★	
17					★			★					★						
18			★					★					★					★	
19						★		★											★
20					★								★						
BONUS PAGES					★	★							★	★	★				
1						★	★						★						
2						★												★	★
3	★					★							★		★				
4						★		★					★						
5						★	★	★					★						
6								★	★										
7								★	★										
8						★		★					★						★
9			★			★		★					★						
10				★				★	★								★		
11				★				★	★				★						
12				★				★					★						
13								★					★						
14					★			★											★
15					★			★					★						
16					★			★									★		
17								★											★
18					★		★	★											★
19							★						★						★
20						★	★						★						
BONUS PAGES		★											★	★	★				★

© Carson Dellosa Education

Summer Reading Ideas

Reading is important all year, not just during school. This summer, set yourself a reading goal and challenge yourself to complete it. You can make your goal one book a month, or even one a week! Choose a goal realistic for you.

Give some of these summer reading ideas a try to make summer reading fun and meaningful.

Read in a New Place
Read in a hammock, under a shady tree, in a sunny spot, on a porch, in a park, in a fort, on a picnic blanket, at a playground, in a tent, or any other spot you've never read before.

Make a Reading List
Make a list of books in a genre you like, books with characters your age, books by your favorite author, or come up with your own list theme. Read as many as you can and check them off as you do.

Read a Summer Book
Choose a book that is summer themed. It could be about a summer trip, summer vacation, a new neighbor, a fun adventure, or set at the beach or in a tropical location.

Be a Chef
Read a cookbook or a book about food. Choose a recipe in the book to make. Write it on a recipe card. Then make it (and enjoy it)! It's up to you if you share it!

Check Your Library
Sign up for your local library's summer reading challenge (or find one online to participate in).

Start a Book Club
Join (or start) a book club with friends or family members. Take turns choosing the book.

Free E-books!
Get started on summer reading fun now by scanning the QR codes for free e-books!

Wild Animal Sanctuaries

Riley Fetter, Star Setter

Rights, Responsibilities, and Conflict

Earth's Landforms

© Carson Dellosa Education

SUMMER READING BINGO

Cross off the reading activities as you do them.

Read under the stars.	Read on a swing.	Read to a stuffed animal or a pet.	Read while eating a frozen treat.	Read on a rainy day.
Read on a Saturday.	Read while eating lunch.	Read with a flashlight.	Read in a pillow fort.	Read in your swimsuit.
Read under a tree.	Read on a Sunday.	FREE	Read to someone on the phone.	Read on a beach towel.
Read in a car.	Read under a table.	Read out loud.	Read to an adult.	Read in your pajamas.
Read at a park.	Read on a Friday.	Read under your covers.	Read a page backwards.	Read in a funny voice.

© Carson Dellosa Education

SECTION 1

Monthly Goals

A goal is something that you want to accomplish. Sometimes, reaching a goal can be hard work!

Think of three goals to set for yourself this month. For example, you may want to read for 30 minutes each day. Write your goals on the lines and review them with an adult.

Place a sticker next to each of your goals that you complete. Feel proud that you have met your goals!

1. _____ PLACE STICKER

2. _____ PLACE STICKER

3. _____ PLACE STICKER

Word List

The following words are used in this section. Read each word. Use a dictionary to look up each word that you do not know. Write two sentences. Use a word from the word list in each sentence.

| coast | flexible | germs | shadow | tame |
| crops | gentle | history | speed | vapor |

1. _____

_____

2. _____

_____

Introduction to Flexibility

This section includes Let's Play Today and Mindful Moments activities that focus on flexibility. These activities are designed to help you become flexible physically and mentally. If you have limited mobility, feel free to modify any suggested activity or choose a different one from the list on the following page.

Let's Play Today

When we talk about flexibility with regard to our bodies, we are referring to how easily our bodies move. If our body isn't flexible, then we will have trouble doing everyday tasks, such as tying our shoes, reaching for things, or playing games or sports.

Over the summer, make a point to stretch regularly to keep your arms and legs moving easily and your back from getting sore. Challenge yourself to touch your toes daily. Did you know that everyday activities, like reaching for a dropped pencil, can practice stretching?

Mindful Moments

Mental flexibility is just as important as physical flexibility. Being mentally flexible means being open-minded. We all know how disappointing it can be when things do not go the way we want them to. Having a fun day at the park ruined because of rain is frustrating. Feeling disappointed or angry as a reaction is normal. In life, there will be situations where unexpected things happen. Often, it is how someone reacts to those circumstances that affects the outcome. It is important to have realistic expectations, brainstorm solutions to improve a disappointing situation, or look on the bright side of a disappointment to find joy even when things do not go as planned.

You can show flexibility of character and mind by being understanding, respecting others' differences, sharing, taking turns, and more. Learning to be flexible now at your age will give you the ability to handle unexpected situations in the years to come.

Engaging Online Practice

Bring learning to life with fun, interactive activities on IXL! Look for the Skill ID box and type the 3-digit code into the search bar on IXL.com or the IXL mobile app. Ten questions per day are free!

IXL Skill IDs: 5UN • D9K

SECTION 1

Let's Play Today

Get up and moving with these Let's Play Today activities. Section 1 focuses on stretching. Stretching helps your body move in its full range of motion and helps you avoid injuring yourself when exercising or playing. Use this list in addition to or as a replacement for any Let's Play Today suggestions on the activity pages. This list was developed to be inclusive of a variety of abilities. Choose the ones that are a good fit for you! Make modifications as needed. These activities may require adult supervision. See page 2 for full caution information.

Bouncy Ball Back-and-Forth:

In an open outdoor space, kick or toss a large bouncy ball back and forth with a friend, family member, or neighbor. Stretch your legs when you kick the ball or lunge to stop a returning ball. Stretch your arms if you are catching it.

The Shallow End Hop:

In the shallow end of a pool, stand on one leg and hold your arms out to your side. Hop from one side of the pool to the other without using your other leg. Switch legs and hop back to the other side.

Stretch to Pop:

Grab a container of bubbles and head outside. Blow bubbles high into the air. Stretch your arms and legs to reach them and pop them before they fall back toward the ground.

Walk a Tightrope:

Use a piece of sidewalk chalk or tape to make a long, thin line on the cement outside. Putting one foot in front of the other and with arms stretched out to the side, slowly walk on the line until you come to the end, being careful to keep your balance. Then turn around and walk back the other way. Try not to step off the line.

Weaving In and Out:

In a yard or at a playground, set up an obstacle course that is made up of traffic cones, toys, or other objects. Start with the objects spread out pretty far, and then move them closer together to make it a little more difficult. Try to move through it without touching any of the objects.

© Carson Dellosa Education

Number Sense/Geometry

Skill IDs: 2R7 • EAQ

DAY 1

Circle the correct numeral for each number word.

1. forty-five
   54   45

2. fifty-eight
   58   85

3. eight hundred eighty-one
   881   81

4. thirty
   30   31

5. three hundred sixty-two
   662   362

6. nine hundred twelve
   921   912

Write the number word for each numeral.

0: _____   20: _____   30: _____

40: _____   60: _____   80: _____

Follow the directions to draw shapes.

7. Draw a shape that has three sides and three angles.

8. Draw a shape with six equal sides and six corners.

9. Draw a shape that has no sides and no corners.

Mindful Moment

Lying on your back, set a small stuffed animal on your chest. Watch it rise and fall as you slowly breathe in and out.

© Carson Dellosa Education

13

DAY 1

Number Sense/Language Arts

Continue each number pattern on the lines. Then, write each rule.

10. 300, 400, 500, 600, _____, _____, _____, _____

    Rule: _____

11. 10, 20, 30, 40, _____, _____, _____, _____, _____, _____

    Rule: _____

12. 5, 10, 15, 20, _____, _____, _____, _____, _____, _____

    Rule: _____

Combine each pair of sentences using the conjunction in parentheses ( ). In each new sentence, place a comma before the conjunction.

13. My grandma raises bees. She has only been stung once. (but)

    My grandma raises bees, but she has only been stung once.

14. Mr. Greene coaches our soccer team. I think he does a great job. (and)

    _____

15. The fireworks lit up the night sky. Everyone cheered. (so)

    _____

16. Tanesha is moving to Illinois. Her family hasn't found a house yet. (but)

    _____

© Carson Dellosa Education

Money/Algebra  DAY 2

Count the money. Write each amount.

1.   _____ ¢

2.    _____ ¢

3.   _____ ¢

4.   _____ ¢

Write the number that the symbol represents in each equation.

5. 🟢 + 5 = 11   🟢 = _____

   Check: 11 − 5 = _____

6. 5 − ⭐ = 2   ⭐ = _____

   Check: 5 − 2 = _____

7. 🟨 + 6 = 14   🟨 = _____

   Check: 14 − 6 = _____

8. 7 + 🔺 = 14   🔺 = _____

   Check: 14 − 7 = _____

© Carson Dellosa Education

15

DAY 2

Phonics

Draw lines to connect syllables to form complete words.

9. pen   met
    sun   cil
    hel   dae

10. rab   der
    spi   bit
    ti   ger

11. pup   en
    can   py
    sev   dy

12. won   ry
    crick   der
    mar   et

13. can   cus
    muf   fin
    cir   dle

14. dol   dow
    mit   lar
    win   ten

15. On the sun, circle the words with *oy*. On the cloud, circle the words with *oi*.

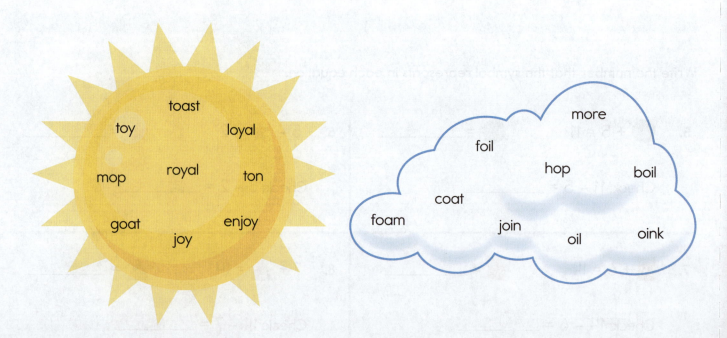

Number Sense/Fractions

Write the number that comes before, between, or after each number or set of numbers.

Before	Between	After
1. _____ 347	4. 213 _____ 215	7. 679 _____
2. _____ 528	5. 427 _____ 429	8. 721 _____
3. _____ 832	6. 399 _____ 401	9. 398 _____

Follow the directions to color equal parts of the shapes.

10. Color one-fourth.
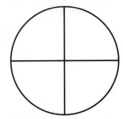

11. Color two-thirds.
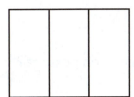

12. Color four-fourths.
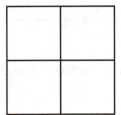

13. Color one-third.
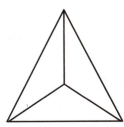

14. Color one-half.
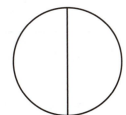

15. Color three-fourths.
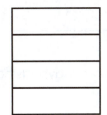

Let's Play Today *See page 12.

Have a crab-walk race with a friend. See who can walk like a crab for the longest or go the farthest.

Helpful Insects and Arachnids

Some insects can destroy crops, such as fruits and vegetables, by eating them. Not all insects are bad though. Some insects help people. Bees move pollen from flower to flower. This helps flowers make seeds so that there will be more flowers the next year. Bees also produce honey. Ladybugs are helpful insects too. They eat the insects that chew on plants. Finally, spiders may look scary, but they are helpful. They are not insects. They are arachnids. They catch flies, crickets, and moths in their webs. If you find a spider in your home, ask an adult to help you carefully place it outside. Then it can do its job outdoors.

16. What is the main idea of this passage?

    A. Insects can destroy crops.

    B. Ladybugs are beautiful.

    C. Some insects and arachnids are helpful.

17. What was the author's purpose in writing this passage?

    _____

18. How do bees help flowers grow?

    _____

19. How are ladybugs helpful?

    _____

20. What are crops? What clues in the passage helped you find the answer?

    _____

Number Sense

 Skill IDs XF9 • 54Z

DAY 4

Write > (greater than) or < (less than) to compare each pair of numbers.

1. 2 ◯ 4   2. 64 ◯ 46   3. 322 ◯ 100

4. 19 ◯ 91   5. 29 ◯ 30   6. 985 ◯ 850

7. 14 ◯ 4   8. 124 ◯ 216   9. 648 ◯ 846

How many are in each group? Write the number on the line. Then, circle *odd* or *even*.

10.

_____   odd   even

11.

_____   odd   even

12.

_____   odd   even

DAY 4

Addition/Phonics

Add to find each sum. Add the numbers in the ones place first. Then add the numbers in the tens place.

13. 3 2
    2 4
    1 1
  +1 9
    8 6

14. 2 8
    1 4
    1 6
  + 4

15. 7 0
    2 6
    9 9
  +1 2

16. 4 4
    4 0
      2
  +3 8

17. 5 7
    3 6
    3 2
  +8 9

18. 8 1
    1 2
    3 8
  +6 4

19. 2 2
    3 4
      9
  +1 9

20. 6 7
    4 1
    4 5
  +1 5

Read each word aloud. Listen to the vowel sounds. If the word has a short vowel sound, write *S* on the line. If the word has a long vowel sound, write *L* on the line.

21. just __S__
22. cape _____
23. clock _____
24. cute _____
25. bug _____
26. ship _____
27. nice _____
28. apple _____
29. goat _____
30. road _____
31. help _____
32. read _____

Number Sense/Fractions

Skill IDs: BDF · QD2

DAY 5

Find the place value of each underlined digit. Circle the answer.

1. 18<u>9</u>	2. <u>2</u>90	3. 1<u>1</u>4
9 hundreds	2 hundreds	1 hundred
9 tens	2 tens	1 ten
(9 ones)	2 ones	1 one
4. 6<u>3</u>4	5. <u>3</u>87	6. 1<u>0</u>9
3 hundreds	3 hundreds	0 hundreds
3 tens	3 tens	0 tens
3 ones	3 ones	0 ones

7. Draw lines to divide the circle into four equal parts.
   What is one part called?

   _____

8. Draw a line to divide the triangle into two equal parts.
   What is one part called?

   _____

9. Draw lines to divide the rectangle into three equal parts.
   What is one part called?

   _____

© Carson Dellosa Education

21

DAY 5

Addition/Phonics

Follow the directions to solve each problem.

10. Start with 15. Write the number that is 10 more. _____

11. Start with 22. Write the number that is 100 more. _____

12. Start with 50. Write the number that is 10 more. _____

13. Start with 335. Write the number that is 100 more. _____

14. Start with 42. Write the number that is 100 more. _____

15. Start with 89. Write the number that is 10 more. _____

Read each word aloud. Then, write *short* or *long* for each vowel sound.

16. bug _____   17. cake _____

18. cut _____   19. street _____

20. road _____   21. catch _____

22. cube _____   23. block _____

24. stick _____   25. child _____

Fast Fun Fact

The White House has its very own movie theater that seats 42 people.

22   © Carson Dellosa Education

Number Sense/Grammar

Circle the number if:

1. 6 is shown in the hundreds place. 629 486 637 926 682 126	2. 9 is shown in the ones place. 879 429 609 191 509 194	3. 3 is shown in the tens place. 231 723 38 639 63 530
4. 5 is shown in the tens place. 354 151 555 185 250 658	5. 4 is shown in the hundreds place. 423 484 124 642 640 432	6. 7 is shown in the ones place. 327 147 607 678 478 447

Words that name holidays, places, and products are proper nouns. Underline the proper noun or nouns in each sentence.

7. Have you ever been to Austin, Texas?

8. Let's do a craft for Hanukkah.

9. My grandmother lives in Iceland.

10. We always buy Papa Pete's pizza when we have family game night.

11. Our neighbors moved here from Nashville, Tennessee.

12. I'd like a glass of orange juice and a bowl of Crunch Os for breakfast.

13. Are you going to wear black, red, and green for Kwanzaa?

Mindful Moment

On a piece of paper, finish this sentence: Three things I like about myself are . . .

Read the passage. Then, answer the questions.

Railroads

Railroads have played an important part in history. For centuries, railroads have helped carry people and goods long distances. In the United States, travel was much harder before a railroad connected the eastern and western parts of the country. Workers in the eastern United States built a railroad heading west. A different crew in the West started building a railroad heading east. In 1869, the two lines met in the state of Utah. The crews hammered in a special golden nail to tie the two tracks together. After that, people could travel easily and quickly from one coast of the United States to the other! The next time you stop at a railroad crossing to let a train pass, think about how important railroads have been in history.

14. What is the main idea of this passage?

  A. Railroads played an important part in history.

  B. No one uses railroads today.

  C. You have to stop to let trains go by.

15. What could people do once the railroad was completed? _____

_____

16. Where did the two railroads begin? _____

17. What did the crews use to join the two tracks? _____

18. The author states that railroads have played an important part in history. Give two reasons from the text that support this point.

_____

_____

Measurement/Grammar

Skill IDs
H5J • DRQ

DAY 7

Find six different books. Measure the length of each book to the nearest inch. Write the measurements below. Then, for each book, draw an *X* above its length on the line plot.

Book 1 _____ inches   Book 2 _____ inches

Book 3 _____ inches   Book 4 _____ inches

Book 5 _____ inches   Book 6 _____ inches

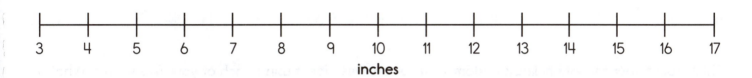

inches

Write each proper noun from the word bank in the correct column.

Memorial Day	Veterans Day
Ukraine	Mexico City
Rocky Mountains	Sweet Orchard fruit
Squeaky Clean soap	St. Louis
Clarabelle's pies	Juneteenth

Holidays   Products   Places

_____   _____   _____

_____   _____   _____

_____   _____   _____

© Carson Dellosa Education

25

DAY 7

Number Sense/Writing

Write each number in expanded form. Show the number as a sum of hundreds, tens, and ones.

1. 528   __500__ + __20__ + __8__
2. 130   _____ + _____ + _____
3. 689   _____ + _____ + _____
4. 421   _____ + _____ + _____
5. 708   _____ + _____ + _____
6. 567   _____ + _____ + _____
7. 963   _____ + _____ + _____
8. 806   _____ + _____ + _____

Think about your favorite holiday, custom, or tradition. Describe it using each of your five senses. What do you see, hear, feel, smell, and taste?

_____

_____

_____

_____

_____

_____

Measurement/Grammar  DAY 8

Measure each object below once to the nearest inch and once to the nearest centimeter. Write the measurements on the lines.

1.    _____ inches

   _____ centimeters

2.    _____ inches

   _____ centimeters

3.    _____ inches

   _____ centimeters

Circle the adverb in each sentence. Then, underline the verb each adverb modifies.

4. The dogs barked loudly at the sound of the garbage truck.

5. I looked everywhere for my coat.

6. Nia swims faster than I do.

7. Greg walked slowly up the driveway.

8. Zahara awoke early on Saturday morning.

9. Let's play outside in the park.

Vocabulary/Phonics

When a prefix is added to a base word, it changes the meaning of the word. Circle the prefix in each word. Then, write the letter of the correct definition next to the word.

10. _____ reopen   A. to wrongly place

11. _____ unhappy   B. not happy

12. _____ misplace   C. to wrongly use

13. _____ unsure   D. to open again

14. _____ misuse   E. not sure

Look at each word. Write how many vowels you see. Then, read each word aloud. Write how many vowel sounds you hear.

	Vowels	Vowel Sounds			Vowels	Vowel Sounds
15. basket	____	____	16. cookies	____	____
17. blocks	____	____	18. alphabet	____	____
19. goat	____	____	20. jump	____	____
21. pilot	____	____	22. lion	____	____
23. radio	____	____	24. carrot	____	____

Let's Play Today *See page 12.

Do a wall sit. Stand with your back facing a wall, then slowly lean against the wall and slide down until you feel like you're sitting in a chair. Hold this pose for 30 seconds.

Addition & Subtraction/Geometry

 Skill IDs NSN • 2VD

DAY 9

Write the related facts for each fact family.

1.

____ + ____ = ____

____ + ____ = ____

____ − ____ = ____

____ − ____ = ____

2.

____ + ____ = ____

____ + ____ = ____

____ − ____ = ____

____ − ____ = ____

3.

____ + ____ = ____

____ + ____ = ____

____ − ____ = ____

____ − ____ = ____

Draw lines to divide each rectangle into rows and columns. Then, count how many squares are in each rectangle and write the number on the line.

4. 3 rows
   5 columns

   How many squares? _____

5. 4 rows
   6 columns

   How many squares? _____

6. 2 rows
   7 columns

   How many squares? _____

© Carson Dellosa Education

Vocabulary/Phonics

When a suffix is added to a base word, it changes the meaning of the word. Add *-less* or *-ness* to the base word in each sentence.

7. The children were very ___rest less___ today.

8. The ___friendli___ of the people made us feel at home.

9. Trying to train my dog to roll over is ___hope___ .

10. The baby loves the ___soft___ of her blanket.

11. The ___loud___ of the noise made me jump.

12. Her ___happi___ showed on her face.

Read each word in the word bank. If the *y* makes the *long i* sound, as in *fly*, write the word under the fly. If the *y* makes the *long e* sound, as in *baby*, write the word under the baby.

| city | dry | eye | happy | sky | story |

fly

baby

_____   _____

_____   _____

_____   _____

Addition & Subtraction

Write the missing sign (+, –, or =) in each number sentence.

1. 6 ___ 3 = 9
2. 12 ___ 6 = 6
3. 4 ___ 2 = 2
4. 4 + 3 ___ 7
5. 14 ___ 1 = 15
6. 12 ___ 2 = 10
7. 9 ___ 3 = 6
8. 14 ___ 4 = 10
9. 14 – 7 ___ 7
10. 4 ___ 1 = 3
11. 7 – 3 ___ 4
12. 3 ___ 3 = 6
13. 8 ___ 4 = 12
14. 9 ___ 2 = 11
15. 11 ___ 2 = 9

Write an addition equation to find the total number of items.

16.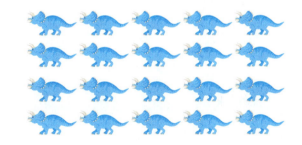
5 + 5 + 5 + 5 = 20

17.
_____

18.
_____

19.
_____

DAY 10

Vocabulary

Underline the compound word in each sentence. Then, draw a line between the two word parts.

20. Rebecca lives on a house|boat.

21. A raindrop hit the white rabbit on the nose.

22. Let's go visit the lighthouse.

23. Did you hear the doorbell ring?

24. The horses are in the barnyard.

25. I cleaned my bedroom this morning.

26. The snowflakes fell very quickly.

Circle the word that matches the definition.

27. to make something bigger

    engage   enrage   enlarge   shrink

28. to like one thing more than another

    decide   buy   prefer   disagree

29. feeling good about something you did

    angry   proud   confused   sad

Fast Fun Fact

The world's longest underwater tunnel, the Seikan Tunnel, is in Japan. It is 33.46 miles long.

32 © Carson Dellosa Education

Problem Solving/Vocabulary

DAY 11

Solve each problem.

1. Dez had 83 marbles. He lost 20 of them. How many marbles does he have left?

2. Armando had 66 apples. He gave 42 apples away. How many apples does Armando have left?

3. Blair walked for 25 minutes. Barack walked for 38 minutes. How many total minutes did the children walk?

4. Nassim saw 18 puppies. Joy saw 49 puppies. How many total puppies did the children see?

Similar words can have different shades of meaning. Circle the word that best completes each sentence.

5. Khalil eagerly (sipped, gulped) the cool water when he got home from his run.

6. The light bulb (shattered, broke) as it hit the floor.

7. "Please don't (gobble, nibble) the popcorn so fast!" exclaimed Dad.

8. Sammy was (furious, mad) that his brand-new bike had been stolen.

9. Rosa (pounded, tapped) on the door, hoping she wouldn't wake the baby.

DAY 11

Vocabulary/Phonics

Read each sentence. Then, write the letter of the underlined word's definition.

10. __B__   The birds can <u>fly</u>.   A.   a small winged insect

      __A__   The spider ate the <u>fly</u>.   B.   to move through the air

11. _____   Please turn on the <u>light</u>.   A.   a lamp

      _____   The box is <u>light</u>.   B.   not heavy

12. _____   <u>Store</u> the books on the shelf.   A.   a place to buy things

      _____   I bought a dress at the <u>store</u>.   B.   to put away for the future

13. _____   Drop a penny in the <u>well</u>.   A.   healthy

      _____   Are you feeling <u>well</u>?   B.   a hole to access underground water

Circle each word that has the /o͞o/ sound, as in *tooth*. Draw an X on each word that has the /o͝o/ sound, as in *hook*.

book	zoo	hoop	wool	cook
hood	soon	pool	scoop	cool
took	stool	food	brook	foot
moon	wood	moose	crook	goose

Mindful Moment

Do an unexpected act of kindness for a friend, family member, or neighbor.

Addition/Spelling

Skill IDs: 5QV • GBG

DAY 12

Draw a line to match the problems that have the same sum.

1.	10 + 3		A.	9 + 2
2.	5 + 6		B.	8 + 8
3.	8 + 4		C.	8 + 5
4.	9 + 7		D.	3 + 6
5.	4 + 5		E.	3 + 7
6.	6 + 4		F.	5 + 13
7.	6 + 9		G.	5 + 9
8.	9 + 8		H.	3 + 9
9.	9 + 9		I.	7 + 8
10.	7 + 7		J.	14 + 3

Use a word from the word bank to write the plural form of each underlined word.

Word Bank: geese, knives, leaves, men, mice, teeth

11. more than one <u>man</u> _____

12. more than one <u>tooth</u> _____

13. more than one <u>leaf</u> _____

14. more than one <u>goose</u> _____

15. more than one <u>knife</u> _____

16. more than one <u>mouse</u> _____

35

DAY 12 — Language Arts/Grammar

Skill ID DVZ — Search for this skill ID on IXL.com for more practice!

17. Write each word from the word bank under the correct heading.

| shirt | pliers | socks | screwdriver | elephant | bear |
| saw | pants | hammer | fox | deer | hat |

Animals   Tools   Clothing

_____   _____   _____

_____   _____   _____

_____   _____   _____

_____   _____   _____

Collective nouns name groups of people, animals, or things. Choose a collective noun from the box to complete each sentence.

| school | swarm | fleet | bouquet | colony |

18. Sophie found a _____ of ants under the rock.

19. A _____ of ships sailed into the harbor.

20. A _____ of bees flew out of the hive.

21. Vijay picked a _____ of flowers for Mom's birthday.

22. Mia saw a _____ of fish swim past the canoe.

© Carson Dellosa Education

Graphing/Language Arts

Study the bar graph. Then, answer each question.

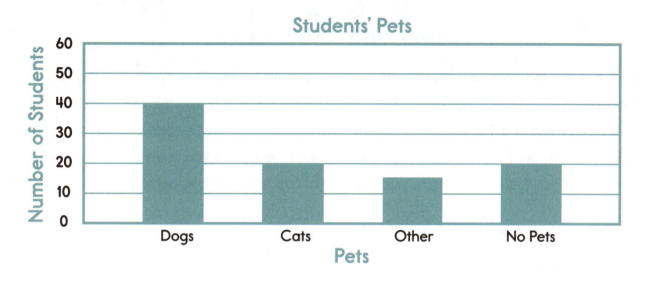

1. How many students have dogs?

   _____

2. How many more students have dogs than cats?

   _____

3. Which two categories have the same amount?

   _____

4. How many students have either a cat or a dog?

   _____

A possessive noun in each sentence is missing an apostrophe. Add an apostrophe like this: Charlotte's kitty.

5. Taylors mask scared her little brother.

6. All of a sudden, the computers screen went blank.

7. Astro chewed up my grandmas slipper.

8. Did you see the piñata at Anas birthday party?

Reading Comprehension

Read the passage. Then, answer the questions.

Washing Your Hands

Your family and teachers have probably told you many times to wash your hands. You should use warm water and soap. Rub your hands together for as long as it takes to sing the alphabet. Then, sing the song again while you rinse your hands. Soap washes off the germs, which are tiny cells that can make you sick. If you do not wash your hands, you can pass a sickness to a friend. Also, you could spread the germs to your eyes or mouth if you touch them before washing your hands. Always remember to wash your hands!

9. What is the main idea of this passage?

   A. Cells can make you sick.

   B. Rub your hands together.

   C. You should wash your hands.

10. How long should you rub your hands together? _____
    _____

11. What does soap do? _____
    _____

12. What does the word *germs* mean?

    A. kind of soap

    B. tiny cells that can make you sick

    C. ways to wash your hands

Let's Play Today *See page 12.

Play your favorite song and dance around to it until it's over.

38 © Carson Dellosa Education

Addition & Subtraction

DAY 14

Add and subtract. Regroup when needed.

1. 635
   +123

2. 987
   −388

3. 457
   +394

4. 108
   +212

5. 852
   −336

6. 754
   −288

7. 808
   + 96

8. 552
   −381

9. 401
   +599

10. 1,000
   − 999

Use the number line to help you solve each problem. Mark the number line to show your work.

11. 60 + 35 = _____

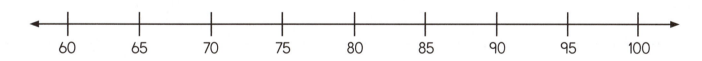

12. 22 + 14 = _____

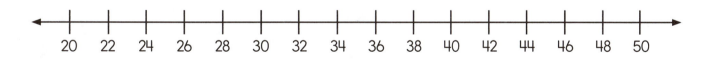

13. 100 − 30 = _____

Search for this skill ID on IXL.com for more practice!

Language Arts/Writing

Read the sentence pairs. Write an *X* beside the sentence that happens first.

14. __X__ I planted seeds.

    _____ The flowers grew.

15. __X__ Luke started his car.

    _____ Luke drove his car.

16. _____ I put on my shoes.

    __X__ I put on my socks.

17. __X__ We built a snowman.

    _____ Our snowman melted.

18. _____ I brushed my teeth.

    __X__ I put toothpaste on my toothbrush.

19. __X__ I climbed into bed.

    _____ I fell asleep.

If you were going to a desert island and could only take three things with you, which three things would you take? Why?

_____

_____

_____

_____

Number Sense/Vocabulary

DAY 15

Write > (greater than), < (less than), or = (equal to) to compare each expression.

1. 7 + 7 < 15
   8 + 6 = 14
   15 > 1 + 9

2. 9 + 7 ◯ 16
   13 − 4 ◯ 10
   4 + 6 ◯ 9

3. 7 + 9 ◯ 18
   17 − 9 ◯ 8
   14 − 4 ◯ 10

4. 8 + 9 ◯ 9 + 8
   11 − 4 ◯ 6 + 2
   16 − 4 ◯ 3 + 10

5. 5 + 8 ◯ 6 + 7
   12 − 6 ◯ 6 + 6
   10 + 1 ◯ 4 + 7

6. 15 − 5 ◯ 13 − 4
   18 − 8 ◯ 8 + 8
   11 + 1 ◯ 6 + 6

Underline the root word in each word. Then, write the definition of the word.

> un- = not   dis- = not, opposite
> re- = again   pre- = before

7. disobey = _____
8. reappear = _____
9. unlucky = _____
10. dishonest = _____
11. preorder = _____
12. unsafe = _____

© Carson Dellosa Education

41

Reading Comprehension

Read the passage. Then, circle the answer that tells what the passage is about.

Birds

All birds are alike in some ways and different in others. They all have wings, but not all of them fly. Some are tame, and some are wild. Some birds sing. Some talk. Some are gentle. Others are not so gentle. Some birds fly very high and far. Others do not. Some birds are colorful, while others are plain.

13. A. Some birds are tame. Others are not.

   B. All birds are strange and colorful.

   C. Birds are alike and different from each other.

Read the passage. Then, circle the answer to the question.

Making Blueberry Muffins

Blueberry muffins are fun and easy to make, and they taste delicious too. The first thing you want to do is set out all of your ingredients. This includes flour, sugar, salt, eggs, butter, blueberries, and a few other things. This makes it easier to follow the directions. The trick to making blueberry muffins that don't turn blue is to fold, or stir, in the blueberries very gently. If you stir them in too hard, they can break open. The juice will leak out and turn the batter blue! Just because they're called blueberry muffins doesn't mean they should be blue. And they taste better when the blueberries are still whole.

14. Why shouldn't you stir the blueberries in too hard?

   A. The batter will become tough.

   B. You will make a big mess.

   C. The batter will turn blue.

One blueberry bush can produce up to 6,000 blueberries every year!

© Carson Dellosa Education

Problem Solving/Measurement

Solve each problem.

1. Kara had 43 flowers. She sold 9 of them. How many flowers does she have left?

2. Alexander can swim 42 laps in one hour. How many laps can he swim in two hours?

3. Miguel has 54 toy cars, and Todd has 22 toy cars. How many more cars does Miguel have than Todd?

4. Latiesha has 19 teddy bears. Brittany has 16 dolls, and Shelby has 8 yo-yos. How many toys do the girls have in all?

5. Samara has a piece of rope that measures 57 centimeters. She cuts off 23 centimeters. How much does she have left?

6. Malia is 54 inches tall. Her little sister is 48 inches tall. How much taller is Malia than her sister?

7. A downtown building is 68 meters tall. A nearby building is 85 meters tall. If you stacked the two buildings, how tall would they be?

8. Grayson has three cats. One weighs 8 pounds, one weighs 14 pounds, and one weighs 17 pounds. How much do his cats weigh altogether?

DAY 16

Reading Comprehension

Read the passage. Then, answer the questions.

The Water Cycle

All water on Earth is part of the same cycle. When the sun heats water in the oceans, lakes, streams, and even in standing water like puddles, drops of water rise into the air. Water in this form is called water vapor. As the air cools, water droplets form clouds. When the clouds become too heavy with water, they produce rain, sleet, hail, or snow. The water falls back to Earth. Some of the water goes into the soil, where it helps plants grow. Some of the water falls back into oceans, lakes, and streams. This cycle happens over and over again. The next time you drink a glass of water, think about where it came from.

9. What is the main idea of this passage?

    A. All water on Earth moves through a cycle.

    B. Think about where your glass of water came from.

    C. Rain moves water back to Earth.

10. What happens when the sun heats the water? _____

11. When do water droplets form clouds? _____

12. What happens when the clouds become too heavy with water? _____
    _____

13. What was the author's purpose for writing this passage? _____
    _____

Mindful Moment

Walk around slowly in a circle. Slowly move your arms up, then down. You're flying like an eagle!

© Carson Dellosa Education

Addition & Subtraction/Grammar

Add or subtract to solve each problem.

1. 84 − 42
2. 37 − 13
3. 69 + 20
4. 18 − 4
5. 57 + 21

6. 28 − 16
7. 24 − 11
8. 10 − 10
9. 23 + 12
10. 26 + 22

11. 43 + 43
12. 91 + 6
13. 15 − 9
14. 12 + 2
15. 49 − 38

Reflexive pronouns are special pronouns that end with *–self* or *–selves*. Circle the reflexive pronoun in each sentence.

16. I told myself that we would have fun, even if it rained.

17. The children were pleased with themselves for finding the hidden treasure.

18. Orin made himself a tasty sandwich.

19. The puppy startled itself when it looked in the mirror.

20. After working all week, Ms. Hayes gave herself the morning off.

DAY 17

Reading Comprehension/Phonics

Read the stories. Decide what will happen next. Then, circle the answers.

21. Beth, Lulu, and Finn were playing at the splash pad. All of a sudden, Lulu fell and hurt her leg.

    A. The kids will all laugh.

    B. The kids will help Lulu out of the splash pad.

    C. The kids will all cry.

22. Jonah was playing soccer with his team. He pushed another player from behind. The referee blew his whistle and held up a red card.

    A. Jonah will be sent to the bench.

    B. Jonah will look exicted.

    C. The other player will get to push Jonah.

Together, the letters *ph* make the /f/ sound. Write the correct word from the word bank to complete each sentence.

| alphabet | amphibian | elephants | phone |

23. What is your _____ number?

24. We saw _____ at the zoo.

25. Omar wrote the letters of the _____ .

26. A frog is an _____ .

46

Addition/Vocabulary

Add to find each sum. Regroup when needed.

1. 324 + 125
2. 973 + 24
3. 477 + 112
4. 206 + 132
5. 384 + 88

6. 420 + 337
7. 688 + 125
8. 621 + 126
9. 442 + 362
10. 175 + 113

11. 767 + 104
12. 603 + 292
13. 398 + 9
14. 300 + 500
15. 525 + 157

Add the prefix *un-* or *re-* to each word. Then, write the meaning of each new word.

16. sure _____

17. happy _____

18. able _____

19. write _____

Writing/Time

If someone is talking face-to-face with another person, do you think they should answer their phone if it rings? Support your opinion with reasons.

_____

_____

_____

Draw hands on each clock to show the correct time. Write the new time where shown.

20.

9:25

21.

5:05

22.

6:35

23.

4:50   _____ : _____

24.  one hour later

11:10   _____ : _____

Let's Play Today *See page 12.

Stand tall and proud. With your arms stretched up over your head, reach for the stars. Then relax your arms. Do this 10 times.

Subtraction/Reading Comprehension

IXL Skill IDs: **55T • VES**

DAY **19**

Subtract to find each difference. Regroup when needed.

1. 724
   −126

2. 410
   −310

3. 833
   −251

4. 978
   −165

5. 811
   −704

6. 701
   −223

7. 583
   −161

8. 900
   −140

9. 683
   −611

10. 896
    −840

Read the fable. Then, answer the questions.

Spilled Milk

A young farmer was going to town to sell her cow's milk. It was a long walk. She amused herself by thinking of what she would do with the money she earned. "I'll buy some laying hens from Farmer Brown," she thought. "And then, I'll sell the eggs they lay to the parson's wife. And with the money I make from the eggs, I'll buy a new dress and a hat to match!"

The farmer was very pleased with the idea of herself in fancy new clothes. *Won't the other girls be jealous*, she imagined. Thinking of this, she tossed her head and spilled the entire pail of milk.

11. What is the moral of this story?

    A. One good turn deserves another.

    B. Look before you leap.

    C. Don't count your chickens before they hatch.

12. What is the purpose of a fable?

    A. to change the reader's mind about something

    B. to teach a lesson

    C. to give directions

© Carson Dellosa Education

49

DAY 19 — Reading Comprehension/Phonics

Read the poem. Then, answer the questions.

My Shadow

I have a little shadow that goes in and out with me,

And what can be the use of him is more than I can see.

He is very, very like me from the heels up to the head;

And I see him jump before me, when I jump into my bed.

– Robert Louis Stevenson

13. What does the boy's shadow do when he jumps into bed? _____
_____

14. Who does the boy's shadow look like? _____

15. Where does the boy's shadow go? _____
_____

16. Clap as you read the poem. Does it have a steady beat? Why? _____
_____

Read each word. Then, circle the letter or letters that are silent.

17. wrist

18. thumb

19. knee

20. knot

21. knight

22. comb

Addition & Subtraction/Grammar

Add or subtract to solve each problem. Regroup when needed.

1. 521
   −132

2. 832
   + 23

3. 153
   +210

4. 612
   −224

5. 638
   −532

6. 34
   +25

7. 288
   + 13

8. 508
   −305

9. 374
   +231

10. 544
   +234

11. 872
   +121

12. 688
   +102

13. 912
   + 87

14. 400
   +500

15. 548
   +292

Write each verb on the correct ladder.

Present — write

blew
blow
find
found
flew
fly
knew

know
laugh
laughed
wear
wore
~~write~~
~~wrote~~

Past — wrote

© Carson Dellosa Education

51

DAY 20

Language Arts/Writing

Write *R* if the sentence tells something that is real. Write *F* if the sentence tells something that is a fantasy.

16. _____ Jennifer wears a watch on her nose.

17. _____ A robin flew to the branch in the tree.

18. _____ Roberto helped his father paint the fence.

19. _____ Danielle heard two trees talking.

20. _____ Kyle eats his lunch with a hammer and a saw.

21. _____ Kayla has two pillows on her bed.

22. _____ Birds use their beaks to fly.

23. _____ Derek lost a baby tooth last night.

24. _____ That cow is driving a bus!

25. _____ The moose gave the frog a cookie.

Imagine that you are designing a T-shirt for a sports team, a school club, or a special event. Draw and color your shirt on another sheet of paper. Describe your shirt.

_____

_____

_____

Fast Fun Fact

There are almost 300 different ways to make change for a dollar.

52 © Carson Dellosa Education

Science Experiment

The Impossible Balloon*

Can you inflate a balloon in a bottle?

Materials:
- balloon
- plastic bottle (2-liter)

Procedure:
With an adult, put the balloon inside the bottle while holding on to the mouth of the balloon. Stretch the mouth of the balloon over the mouth of the bottle so that it stays in place. Then, put your lips on the bottle. Try to inflate the balloon.

What's This All About?
When you stretch the balloon over the mouth of the bottle, it seals the bottle. No air can get in or out of the bottle. As you try to inflate the balloon, it pushes against the air inside the bottle. The air pushes on the balloon and does not let the balloon get any bigger. Air takes up space and can push things that push it.

More Fun Ideas to Try:
- Try different sizes of bottles to see if you can inflate the balloon in other bottles.
- Try round balloons or long balloons. Before you try the experiment, write what you think might happen.
- Have an adult punch a small hole in the bottom of a bottle. Try the experiment with this bottle.
- Write a letter or an e-mail to a friend or relative. Tell about the experiment you did. Explain how it works and what your results were.

Think About It:
- What is the *mouth* of the balloon? What is the *mouth* of the bottle?
- Which section of the experiment tells you what to do, step by step?

Write About It:
If you tried this experiment with a bottle that has a tiny hole in it (as suggested above), what happened? If you haven't tried it, what do you think would happen?

_____

_____

*See page 2.

Search for this skill ID on IXL.com for more practice!

BONUS

Science Experiment

Fluid Motion

Will the same object move at different speeds through different fluids?

Speed is the term used to describe how fast an object moves. To calculate speed, divide the distance the object moved by how much time it took to move.

Materials:
- 2 identical jars
- vegetable oil
- stopwatch
- calculator
- water
- two identical marbles
- metric ruler

Procedure:
Fill one jar with water and one jar with vegetable oil.

Hold one marble so that the bottom of the marble touches the top of the vegetable oil. Drop the marble. Use the stopwatch to record the time in seconds that it takes the marble to reach the bottom of the jar. Then, use the ruler to measure the distance the marble traveled. Record your data in the chart.

Follow the same procedure for the second marble and the jar of water. Record your data in the chart.

Divide the distance that each marble traveled by the number of seconds it took for that marble to drop. Use a calculator if you need help.

Measurements			
Fluid	Distance	Time	Speed
vegetable oil			
water			

Which marble traveled faster? _____

What is the difference between the speed of the two marbles? _____

54 © Carson Dellosa Education

Social Studies Activity

X Marks the Spot

Follow the directions to find the treasure. Draw an *X* where the treasure is buried. Then, answer the question.

- Start in the Red River Valley.
- Go northeast through Lake Lavender to the Black Forest.
- Go northeast to the Evergreen Forest.
- Travel north to the Purple Mountains.
- Cross the Red River to the Blue Mountains.
- Go south, but do not cross the Red River again.
- The treasure is buried here.

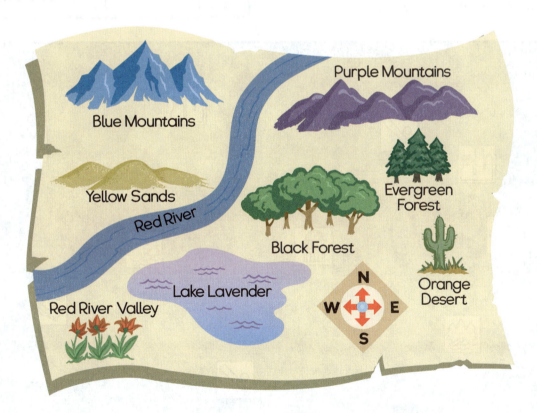

Where is the treasure buried? _____

55

Social Studies Activity

What's the Key?

A map key tells what the symbols on a map stand for. Use the map key to find the objects listed.

1. Circle each city.

2. Draw a square around each baseball park.

3. Draw an X on the state capitol.

4. Draw a triangle around the airport.

5. Underline the parks.

6. Draw a star on each university.

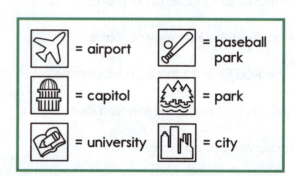

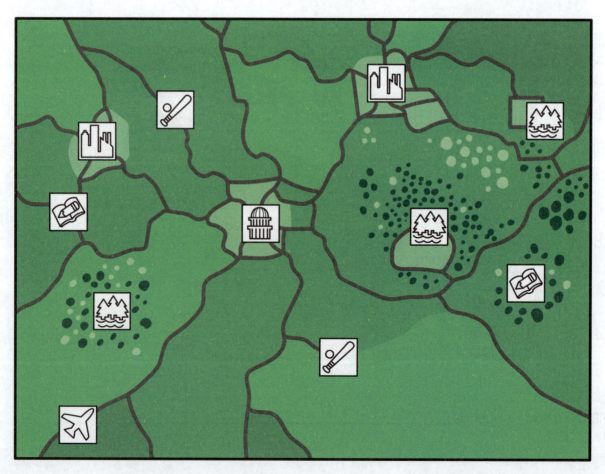

56 © Carson Dellosa Education

Social Studies Activity

Bryant's Street Map

Bryant has a street map to help him find his way around his new town. A street map shows where businesses, homes, and other places are located. Look at the street map and answer the questions.

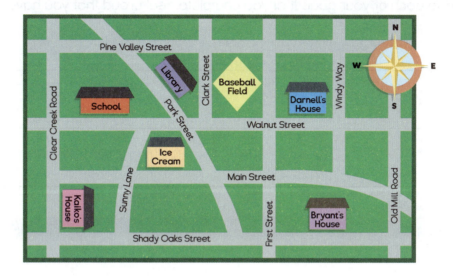

1. Bryant lives on _____.

2. Kaiko lives on _____.

3. The ice-cream shop is on _____.

4. Darnell lives at the corner of Walnut Street and _____.

5. The school is on _____.

6. What two streets could Bryant take to get to the library from his house?

   _____

© Carson Dellosa Education

57

SECTION 2

Monthly Goals

Think of three goals to set for yourself this month. For example, you may want to exercise for 20 minutes each day. Write your goals on the lines and review them with an adult.

Place a sticker next to each of your goals that you complete. Feel proud that you have met your goals!

1. _____ PLACE STICKER

2. _____ PLACE STICKER

3. _____ PLACE STICKER

Word List

The following words are used in this section. Read each word. Use a dictionary to look up each word that you do not know. Then, write two sentences. Use a word from the word list in each sentence.

| advertising | illustrated | nectar | published | seasons |
| cabin | molt | popular | recycle | tropical |

1. _____

_____

2. _____

_____

58 © Carson Dellosa Education

Introduction to Strength

This section includes Let's Play Today and Mindful Moments activities that focus on strength. These activities are designed to help you spend less time on a screen and more time developing healthy emotional and physical habits. If you have limited mobility, feel free to modify any suggested activity or choose a different one from the list on the following page.

Let's Play Today

Like flexibility, strength is necessary to be healthy. You might think being strong means lifting an enormous amount of weight. But strength is much more than just the ability to pick up heavy barbells. Strength is built by being physically active on a daily basis. As a toddler, you walked down the sidewalk. Now you can run across a baseball field. Look how strong you've become!

Everyday activities, fun exercises, and enjoyable games help you gain strength. Take a walk, do a classic exercise such as push-ups, or play a game of basketball or tag to build your physical strength.

Set realistic, achievable goals to improve your physical strength based on your ability and the activities you enjoy. Over the summer months, keep track of these goals and celebrate when you achieve them. Then set new ones!

Mindful Moments

Having strength of character on the inside is just as important as having physical strength on the outside. Being a strong person on the inside can be shown by being honest, facing a fear, helping others, standing up for someone who needs a friend, or choosing to do the right thing when presented with a difficult situation. Think about times when you have had inner strength that has helped you handle a situation.

Engaging Online Practice

Bring learning to life with fun, interactive activities on IXL! Look for the Skill ID box and type the 3-digit code into the search bar on IXL.com or the IXL mobile app. Ten questions per day are free!

Skill IDs: 5UN • D9K

SECTION 2

Let's Play Today

Get your child up and moving with these Let's Play Today activities. Section 2 focuses on strength. Strengthening exercises make your bones and muscles stronger. Strong bones and muscles help prevent injury and speed up recovery from injury. Use this list in addition to or as a replacement for any Let's Play Today suggestions on the activity pages. This list was developed to be inclusive of a variety of abilities. Choose the ones that suit your child the best! Make modifications as needed. These activities may require adult supervision. See page 2 for full caution information.

Lava Pit:
Hop from pillow to pillow on an imaginary bed of lava. Start with just 3-4 pillows and repeat it two times. Over time, gradually add pillows to work up to a longer, more complex path of pillows. Repeat hopping on the longer path 10 times.

Frog Hops:
Crouch down with your hands on the floor in a frog-like position. Hop forward like a frog 3-4 times. Over time, gradually increase the number of hops until you get to 15.

Shadow Fun:
Go outside on a sunny day and stand so you can see your shadow. If you are by yourself, practice shadow boxing. Bend your arms at the elbows and bring your hands back to your body. Make a fist with each hand. Extend one arm at a time to mimic a boxing motion. If someone is outside with you, trace each other's shadow with sidewalk chalk. Hold a pose that works your muscles, such as standing on one leg or flexing your arms.

Balloon Back-and-Forth:
Either seated or standing, hit a balloon up into the air to another person. That person will hit it back to you. Keep track of how many times you can hit it to each other without it touching the ground. Try to increase your score.

Swim Like a Fish:
Wearing a life jacket in the shallow end of a pool, try swimming like a fish. Use flippers to help. See how many different ways to swim you can come up with. For example, swim like you have a fish tail, swim without using your arms, swim with flippers on your hands, or roll around.

60 © Carson Dellosa Education

Addition/Grammar

Add to find each sum.

1. 63 + 48
2. 47 + 68
3. 19 + 28
4. 55 + 59
5. 24 + 87

6. 64 + 18
7. 72 + 48
8. 48 + 64
9. 37 + 95
10. 27 + 56

11. 16 + 34
12. 33 + 8
13. 46 + 78
14. 19 + 39
15. 28 + 67

Draw a line to match each present-tense verb with its past-tense form.

16. sleep   held
17. hold   fell
18. make   left
19. win   bought
20. leave   slept
21. fall   made
22. buy   won

Language Arts/Spelling

Rewrite each set of underlined words as a possessive.

23. The baseball mitt belonging to Dion is on the dresser. _____

24. Have you seen the soccer ball belonging to Jasper? _____

25. I forgot to bring the goggles belonging to Trinity. _____

26. The golf clubs belonging to Grandpa are in the basement. _____

27. The ballet shoes belonging to Cassidy are too small. _____

Read the sentences. Look at each underlined word. Then, color in the circle to tell if the word is spelled correctly or incorrectly.

		CORRECT	INCORRECT
28.	We ate toast with jam on it.	●	○
29.	We wint to the store for some bread and milk.	○	○
30.	The dog will hunt for his boone.	○	○
31.	We will plant our garden.	○	○
32.	The keng asked the queen to dance.	○	○

Mindful Moment

Think of someone whom you admire. Draw a picture of the two of you together. Give it to that person.

Subtraction/Grammar

DAY 2

Subtract to find each difference. Subtract the numbers in the ones place first. Then subtract the numbers in the tens place.

1. 51
   −38
   ___

2. 75
   −26
   ___

3. 82
   −37
   ___

4. 27
   −19
   ___

5. 65
   − 9
   ___

6. 83
   −24
   ___

7. 95
   −78
   ___

8. 56
   −17
   ___

9. 81
   − 6
   ___

10. 54
   −39
   ___

11. 64
   −18
   ___

12. 35
   −16
   ___

Write the past-tense form of each verb to complete each sentence.

13. Chang _____ a card for Alfonso.
    (make)

14. Lindsey _____ her cat to the vet.
    (take)

15. She _____ enough bread for a week.
    (buy)

16. Claire and I _____ the movie last night.
    (see)

17. I _____ to the gas station.
    (go)

18. The bird _____ to the nest.
    (fly)

© Carson Dellosa Education

63

DAY 2

Search for this skill ID on IXL.com for more practice!

Reading Comprehension

Read the poem. Then, answer the questions.

Sing a Song of Summer

Sing a song of summer
with arms stretched open wide.
Run in the sunshine.
Play all day outside.

Hold on to the summer
as long as you may.
Autumn will come quickly
and shorten the day.

Play in the water.
Roll in the grass.
It won't be long now
before you'll be in class.

19. Which sentence tells the main idea of the poem?

    A. Enjoy summer while it lasts.   B. Summer gets too hot.

    C. School starts in the autumn.   D. It is fun to sing songs.

20. What season comes after summer?

    A. winter   B. spring

    C. autumn   D. October

21. Write an X beside each thing you can do in the summer.

    _____ play outside   _____ rake leaves

    _____ go swimming   _____ build a snowman

64 © Carson Dellosa Education

Addition & Subtraction/Grammar Skill IDs YZ2 • Z7Y

DAY 3

Add or subtract to solve each problem.

1. 433
    + 18

2. 762
    − 28

3. 819
    + 20

4. 453
    − 5

5. 658
    + 24

6. 544
    − 18

7. 234
    − 9

8. 372
    + 9

9. 675
    − 47

10. 981
    + 11

Write *am*, *is*, or *are* to complete each sentence.

11. I _____ the tallest girl on the team.

12. My lunch _____ in my backpack.

13. We _____ in line for the roller coaster.

14. I _____ ready to go swimming.

15. Jonah's friends _____ laughing at a joke.

16. Aunt Ebony _____ listening to music.

17. We _____ painting the room blue.

 **Let's Play Today** *See page 60.

Lie on your back with your legs in the air. Move your legs like you are riding a bike for one minute.

© Carson Dellosa Education   65

Write a multiplication equation to show the number of items in each group.

18.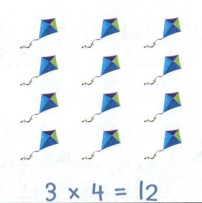
3 × 4 = 12

19.

20.

21.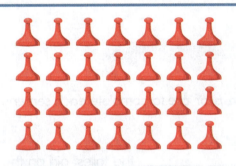

Multiply.

22. 5
    ×2

23. 3
    ×2

24. 1
    ×7

25. 8
    ×2

26. 4
    ×2

27. 2
    ×2

28. 5 × 5 =

29. 3 × 3 =

30. 2 × 2 =

Measurement/Grammar

Find the area of each figure.

1.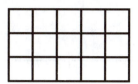

   _____ × _____ = _____
   base   height   total area

2.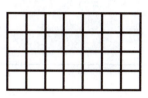

   _____ × _____ = _____
   base   height   total area

3.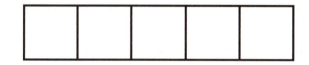

   _____ × _____ = _____
   base   height   total area

4.

   _____ × _____ = _____
   base   height   total area

Look at each underlined word. On the line, write whether it is a noun, pronoun, verb, adjective, or adverb.

5. _____ The gray <u>tent</u> smelled of leaves and woodsy air.

6. _____ Grandpa <u>quickly</u> unzipped the tent's windows.

7. _____ The smell of <u>crispy</u> bacon filled the air.

8. _____ A cool stream <u>ran</u> along one side of the campsite.

9. _____ <u>I</u> couldn't wait to start the campfire.

10. _____ We <u>roasted</u> six ears of corn.

© Carson Dellosa Education

67

DAY 4 — Fractions/Language Arts

Mark each fraction on the number line.

11. 3/4

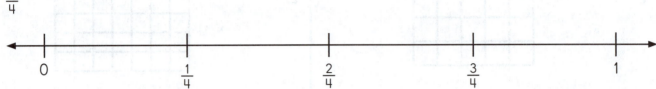

12. 5/8

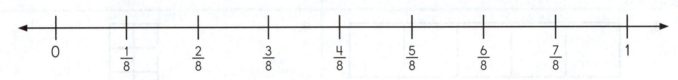

13. 1/3

14. 10/10 or 1 whole

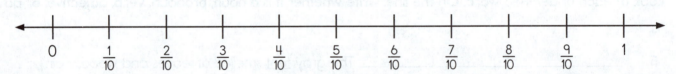

Add the missing commas to each address below. Use this symbol to add them: ⸴ .

81 Riverwood Rd.
Charlotte NC 28870

1425 Newtown Terrace #12
Providence RI 02906

132 West Billingsley Lane
Taos NM 87571

21896 Langston Blvd.
San Diego CA 92119

Addition & Subtraction/Grammar

 Skill IDs
WXQ • EG2

DAY 5

Use a red pencil to check the problems. Write a ✓ beside each correct answer. Write an X beside each incorrect answer.

1. 423
   +138
   ─────
    561

2. 784
   −107
   ─────
    618

3. 434
   +128
   ─────
    562

4. 324
   +267
   ─────
    592

5.   38
    +19
   ─────
     57

6. 667
   −419
   ─────
    247

7. 410
   −125
   ─────
    305

8. 948
   −819
   ─────
    129

9. 546
   −317
   ─────
    218

10. 634
   −571
   ─────
     63

11. 342
   −237
   ─────
    105

12. 467
   +161
   ─────
    628

Write *has* or *have* to complete each sentence.

13. We _____ fun plans for this summer.

14. My mom _____ Friday off.

15. My friends _____ a new game to play.

16. The boy _____ a broken leg.

 **Fast Fun Fact**

Maine is the only state that has a one-syllable name.

Reading Comprehension/Writing

Read the passage. Then, answer the questions.

Mercer Mayer

Mercer Mayer's books can be found in many libraries and bookstores. He has both written and illustrated books. Some of his most popular books include *There's a Nightmare in My Closet*; *Liza Lou and the Yeller Belly Swamp*; *Just for You*; and *A Boy, a Dog, and a Frog*. He likes to write about things that happened to him as a child.

Mercer Mayer was born on December 30, 1943, in Arkansas. When he was 13, he moved to Hawaii with his family. After high school, he studied art. Then, he worked for an advertising company in New York. He published his first book in 1967. He and his wife work together on the Little Critter stories. Now, he works from his home in Connecticut.

17. This passage is called a *biography*. Based on what you read, what do you think a biography is?

    A. a made-up story about a character from a book

    B. a true story that tells about the life of a real person

    C. a short, funny story

Write *T* for statements that are true. Write *F* for statements that are false.

18. _____ Mercer Mayer is a character in a book.

19. _____ Mercer Mayer writes about things that happened to him as a child.

20. _____ Mercer Mayer lived in many different places.

21. _____ Mercer Mayer never worked in New York.

22. Do some research on another children's author. On a separate piece of paper, write a paragraph about the author you chose. How is the author similar to Mercer Mayer? How is the author different from him?

Time/Vocabulary

Write the time shown on each clock.

1.

   _____ : _____

2.

   _____ : _____

3.

   _____ : _____

4.

   _____ : _____

5.

   _____ : _____

6.

   _____ : _____

Use the prefix and suffix meanings in the box to help you write a definition for each word.

un–/non– = not	-er/or = one who
re– = again	-tion = the result of
dis– = not, opposite of	-ness = state of being

7. gardener = _____

8. dishonest = _____

9. addition = _____

10. nonstick = _____

11. unhealthy = _____

12. illness = _____

13. collector = _____

14. reuse = _____

DAY 6 — Vocabulary/Writing

Circle the root word in each item. Then, think of another word that has the same root. Write the new word on the line.

15. unreasonable _____

16. disinterested _____

17. misbehaving _____

18. unbelievable _____

19. bicycling _____

20. telephone _____

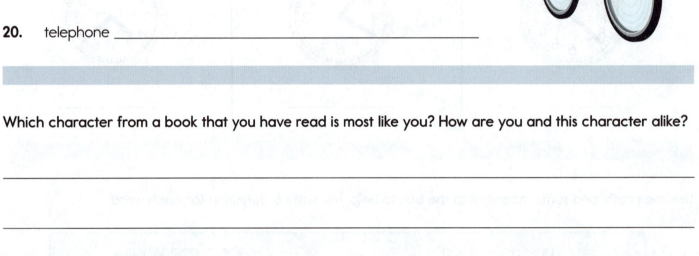

Which character from a book that you have read is most like you? How are you and this character alike?

_____

_____

_____

_____

Mindful Moment

Finish this sentence:
Something new that I have learned how to do recently is …
Tell a friend or family member about it.

Time/Vocabulary

DAY 7

Draw hands on each clock to show the correct time.

1.
12:45

2.
9:17

3.
12:31

4.
8:28

5.
5:40

6.
12:09

Add the suffixes *-ed* and *-ing* to each base word. You may need to drop letters from or add letters to some words before adding the suffixes.

7. rake

8. jump

9. hug

10. cook

11. skate

_____   _____   _____   _____   _____

_____   _____   _____   _____   _____

12. wrap

13. sneeze

14. pop

15. talk

16. smile

_____   _____   _____   _____   _____

_____   _____   _____   _____   _____

© Carson Dellosa Education

73

DAY 7

Vocabulary/Measurement

Write the letter of the correct definition next to each word.

17. _____ cheerful   A. ready to help

18. _____ sleepless   B. without sun

19. _____ colorful   C. very cheery

20. _____ sunless   D. having many colors

21. _____ helpful   E. not able to sleep

Perimeter is the distance all the way around a shape. Write the perimeter of each figure.

22.
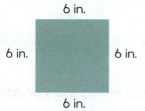

perimeter = _____ in.

23.
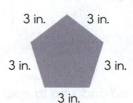

perimeter = _____ in.

24.
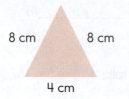

perimeter = _____ cm

25.
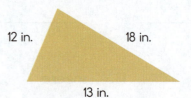

perimeter = _____ in.

Time/Grammar

Solve the word problems about time.

1. Felipe got on the bus at 7:30. It took him 20 minutes to get to school. What time did he arrive?

   _____

2. Aliya's piano lesson started at 4:15. It lasted half an hour. What time did she finish her lesson?

   _____

3. It started raining at 6:05. It rained for 45 minutes. What time did it stop raining?

   _____

4. Mr. Domingo's class got to the museum at 9:00. They left two-and-a-half hours later. What time did they leave?

   _____

Write the word *went* or *gone* to complete each sentence. Hint: The word *gone* needs another word to help it, such as *has* or *will be*.

5. Ben _____ home after school.

6. Jessi has _____ shopping for a new coat.

7. Deanna _____ with Andrew to play.

8. We will be _____ on vacation all week.

DAY 8 — Reading Comprehension

Read the passage. Then, answer the questions.

Nightly Navigators

Bats help people in many ways. Most bats eat insects at night. This helps to keep the number of insects low. Bats eat mosquitoes, mayflies, and moths. Bats also pollinate and spread the seeds of many tropical trees.

Bats are the only mammals on Earth that fly by flapping their limbs. There are more than 900 kinds of bats. Some bats are only 1.3 inches (3.3 centimeters) long. Some are more than 16 inches (40 centimeters) long. Most bats eat only insects. Some bats eat fruit and the nectar of flowers.

9. How many different kinds of bats are there? _____

10. What do bats eat? _____

11. How large can some types of bats grow? _____

12. What is the main idea of the first paragraph? _____
_____

13. What evidence does the author give that supports the main idea in the first paragraph?
_____
_____

14. Name three types of insects that bats eat. _____

Let's Play Today *See page 60.*

Bend over as if you are touching your toes. With your hands clasped together, sway your arms back and forth like an elephant sways its trunk. Do this for one minute.

76 © Carson Dellosa Education

Money/Grammar

Circle the coins to equal each amount shown.

1. 34¢

2. 72¢

3. 25¢

4. 49¢

Write a word from each box to complete each sentence.

5. The train will _____ .

   The train is _____ .

   The train has _____ .

   | stop |
   | stopped |
   | stopping |

6. The baby can _____ .

   The baby is _____ .

   The baby _____ .

   | clap |
   | clapped |
   | clapping |

7. The rabbit is _____ .

   The rabbit _____ .

   The rabbit can _____ .

   | hop |
   | hopped |
   | hopping |

Number Sense

Round each number to the nearest ten.

8. 56 _____

9. 142 _____

10. 33 _____

11. 289 _____

12. 11 _____

Round each number to the nearest hundred.

13. 342 _____

14. 586 _____

15. 204 _____

16. 650 _____

17. 817 _____

For each number, circle whether it is even or odd.

18. 235 even odd	19. 88 even odd	20. 910 even odd
21. 501 even odd	22. 38 even odd	23. 99 even odd
24. 100 even odd	25. 1 even odd	26. 763 even odd

Graphing/Grammar

Mr. Cohen is tracking how many loaves of bread his bakery has sold each month so far this year. Fill in the pictograph below based on the following data for each month.

January = 40 loaves
February = 40 loaves
March = 60 loaves
April = 80 loaves
May = 85 loaves
June = 95 loaves

Month	Loaves of Bread Sold
January	
February	
March	
April	
May	
June	

Key: ⌂ = 10 loaves

Cross out each incorrectly used or misspelled word in the journal entry. Write the correct word above it.

September 14, 2024

Yesterday, we learn about colors in art. We make a color wheel. We found out that there is three basic colors. They am called *primary colors*. Red, yellow, and blue are primary colors. Primary colors mix to make other colors. Red and yellow makes orange. Yellow and blue make green. Blue and red make purple. Orange, green, and purple is secondary colors.

DAY 10 — Vocabulary/Multiplication

Circle the meaning of each underlined word.

1. She has on a <u>dark</u> purple dress.
   - A. night
   - B. not light

2. We were <u>safe</u> on the rock.
   - A. without danger
   - B. place to keep things

3. Fernando had to be home before <u>dark</u>.
   - A. morning
   - B. night

4. I took a <u>trip</u> to the aquarium.
   - A. a visit
   - B. to stumble

5. The <u>bank</u> closes at five o'clock.
   - A. a place where money is kept
   - B. a steep hill

Solve each problem.

6. 20 × 9
7. 50 × 7
8. 90 × 4
9. 80 × 3
10. 40 × 6

11. 30 × 9
12. 60 × 8
13. 10 × 8
14. 20 × 3
15. 70 × 1

Fast Fun Fact

Your heart beats about 115,000 times per day.

Money/Grammar

Count the groups of money in each problem. Draw an *X* on the group that is worth more.

1.   2.

3.   4.

Adjectives describe nouns. Write the best adjective from the word bank to complete each sentence.

| rainy | equal | low | tiny |

5. I put an _____ amount of soup in my bowl and yours.

6. There is a _____ bug on the leaf.

7. Latoya stepped over the _____ wall.

8. She saw a rainbow in the sky on the _____ day.

DAY 11

Reading Comprehension

Read the passage. Then, answer the questions.

Continents

Earth has seven continents: Africa, Antarctica, Asia, Australia, Europe, North America, and South America. These continents were once a large piece of land. The land split millions of years ago. Large pieces of land drifted apart. The oceans filled the spaces between the pieces of land. The continents we know today are the result. Each continent looks different and has different plants, animals, and weather. North America does not have tigers, but Asia does. Antarctica does not have a jungle, but South America does. The continents are similar in some ways. Some similarities may be because the continents were once one large piece of land.

9. What is the main idea of this passage?

   A. Earth is made of land and water.

   B. Earth has seven continents that were once one piece of land.

   C. Earth has many types of animals, plants, and weather.

10. List the seven continents. _____
    _____

11. When did the continents form? _____

12. Why might continents with an ocean between them have similarities?
    _____
    _____

Mindful Moment

On a piece of paper, draw an outline of a body. Next to the ears, eyes, mouth, and hands, write how they bring you joy, such as, "My ears help me hear my friends' voices."

82 © Carson Dellosa Education

Money/Grammar  DAY 12

Make one dollar in change five different ways.

1.	quarters	2	2.	quarters	___	3.	quarters	___
	dimes	4		dimes	___		dimes	___
	nickels	2		nickels	___		nickels	___
	pennies	0		pennies	___		pennies	___
	total	$ 1.00		total	$ ___		total	$ ___

4.	quarters	___	5.	quarters	___	6.	quarters	___
	dimes	___		dimes	___		dimes	___
	nickels	___		nickels	___		nickels	___
	pennies	___		pennies	___		pennies	___
	total	$ ___		total	$ ___		total	$ ___

Circle the adjectives in each sentence.

7. The (big) (red) wagon rolled down the hill.

8. Joaquin likes a soft pillow.

9. The hikers climbed a steep hill.

10. The door made a screechy noise.

Search for this skill ID on IXL.com for more practice!

Number Sense/Writing

Round each number to the nearest ten and nearest hundred. Then, write each number in expanded form.

		Ten	Hundred	Expanded Form
11.	256	260	300	200 + 50 + 6
12.	542			
13.	311			
14.	898			
15.	426			
16.	657			
17.	102			

Think about something that you could reuse or recycle. How would you reuse or recycle it?

_____

_____

_____

_____

Problem Solving/Grammar

It takes two steps to find the solution to each problem below. Write both equations you use to find each solution.

1. Ezra has $20. He buys 3 fossils for $3 each. How much money does he have left?

   3 × $3 = $9 $20 − $9 = $11

2. Fiona had a garden party with 6 friends. Each friend got 2 packets of flower seeds to take home. Fiona kept 4 packets of seeds for her own garden. How many packets of flower seeds were there in all?

   _____

3. Azim had 55 grapes. He fed his 8 chickens 6 grapes each. How many grapes were left?

   _____

4. Byron's mom makes picnic blankets. She can make 9 blankets with 27 yards of fabric. How much fabric would she need to make 12 blankets?

   _____

Circle the adjectives that describe each underlined noun.

5. I have a blue and yellow <u>dress</u>.

6. The little green <u>snake</u> climbed the tree.

7. Tasha made a towel from colorful, soft <u>cloth</u>.

8. The dark gray <u>cloud</u> is over my house.

9. I wore my new brown <u>sandals</u> today.

Reading Comprehension

Read the story. Then, number the events in the order that they happened.

Snowed In

It snowed for three days. When it stopped, the snow was so deep that Ivan and Jacob could not open the cabin door. The men climbed through the upstairs window to get outside. They spent hours shoveling the snow away from the door. At last, they could open the door.

10. _____ The men climbed out the window.

    _____ It snowed for three days.

    _____ Ivan and Jacob opened the door.

    _____ The men shoveled snow for hours.

For each sentence, circle whether it is a fact or an opinion.

11.	Chicken noodle soup is delicious!	fact	opinion
12.	Some types of soup are served cold.	fact	opinion
13.	Spicy black bean soup is too spicy.	fact	opinion
14.	January is National Soup Month.	fact	opinion

Let's Play Today *See page 60.*

Jump into the air to make a starfish shape. Extend both legs and both arms in different directions. Repeat 10 times.

86 © Carson Dellosa Education

Measurement/Writing

Measure each line segment to the closest inch. Write the measurements in the boxes. Then, add the measurements.

1.

   ☐ + ☐ + ☐ = _____ inches

2.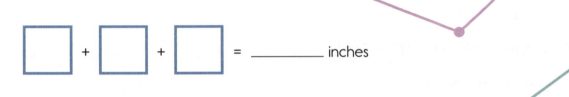

   ☐ + ☐ + ☐ = _____ inches

3.

   ☐ + ☐ + ☐ = _____ inches

Start a story about a character who does something for the first time. Maybe the person is starting a new school or joining a soccer team. Continue your story on another piece of paper.

_____

_____

_____

_____

Reading Comprehension

Read the passage. Then, answer the questions.

Sleep

Are you ever sleepy in the middle of the day? Children need about 8 to 11 hours of sleep each night. During sleep, your body rests and gets ready for another day. It is important to be rested for school every morning. If you are tired, you might have trouble paying attention to your teacher. If you have a hard time falling asleep, try reading a book instead of watching TV before bedtime. Go to bed at the same time every night. Play soft music to help you get sleepy. Soon, you will be dreaming!

4. What is the main idea of this passage?

   A. Getting enough sleep is important.

   B. Reading a book can help you go to sleep.

   C. You should dream every night.

5. How much sleep do children need? _____

6. What might happen at school if you are tired? _____
   _____

7. What can you do instead of watching TV at bedtime? _____
   _____

8. When should you go to bed?

   A. 10 P.M.

   B. only when you feel sleepy

   C. at the same time every night

Measurement/Grammar

Measure the length of each object in centimeters.

1. _____ cm

2. _____ cm

3. _____ cm

4. _____ cm

5. _____ cm

Write an adjective to complete each sentence.

6. Gabriel showed me the _____ picture.

7. The _____ puppy is chasing his tail.

8. That _____ bird flies south for the winter.

9. Colby carried the _____ suitcase.

10. That book with the _____ cover is mine.

Reading Comprehension/Writing

Circle the letter next to the main idea of each paragraph.

11. Sometimes I have strange dreams. Once, I dreamed I was floating inside a spaceship. When I woke up, I thought I was still floating. I reminded myself that it was just a dream. When I told my mom about it, she said that she sometimes has strange dreams, too.

    A. I dreamed I was floating in space.

    B. My mom had the same dream I did.

    C. Sometimes, we have strange dreams.

12. I like to read. In the summer, I go to the library twice a week. I check out books about lemurs and airplanes. I also like to read about rainforests. The librarian helps me find books I will like.

    A. I read books about race cars in the summer.

    B. I find books to read at the library.

    C. Librarians are friendly and helpful.

Start a story about a character who does a good deed. Finish it on another piece of paper. Share it with a friend or family member.

_____

_____

_____

_____

Fast Fun Fact

The longest word in the English language without any vowels is *rhythms*.

90 © Carson Dellosa Education

Measurement/Language Arts

One meter is 100 centimeters. Circle your estimate for each question.

1. A dictionary is
   A. taller than one meter.
   B. (shorter than one meter.)

2. A house is
   A. taller than one meter.
   B. shorter than one meter.

3. A baby is
   A. longer than one meter.
   B. shorter than one meter.

4. Your front door is
   A. taller than one meter.
   B. shorter than one meter.

5. A pencil is
   A. longer than one meter.
   B. shorter than one meter.

6. A paper clip is
   A. longer than one meter.
   B. shorter than one meter.

Write the contraction for each set of words.

7. has not ___hasn't___
8. I am _____
9. you will _____
10. would not _____
11. we have _____
12. we would _____
13. you are _____
14. she is _____
15. is not _____
16. I willl _____

DAY 16

Search for these skill IDs on IXL.com for more practice!

Language Arts/Spelling

Use the table of contents to answer the questions.

17. On which page should you begin reading about where ants live?

   _____

18. Which chapter would tell about the different kinds of ants?

   _____

Table of Contents
Chapter 1: All About Ants 1
Chapter 2: Where Ants Live 4
Chapter 3: Types of Ants 6
Chapter 4: Ant Anatomy 11
Chapter 5: What Ants Do 16
Chapter 6: Ant Families 21
Index 26

19. On which page would you look to find the index?

   _____

20. What is the title of the first chapter?

   _____

Draw an *X* over each misspelled word. Write each word correctly.

21. Marcus has a new electrik car.   _____

22. Bonnie takes the fast trane to work.   _____

23. Let's keap our group together.   _____

24. My dad drives a large dump truk.   _____

25. Let's plae baseball.   _____

Mindful Moment

How are you feeling today? Why are you feeling this way? Choose one word to describe your mood. Draw a picture to go along with the word you chose.

92   © Carson Dellosa Education

Measurement/Language Arts

Estimate the volume of each item. Circle your answer.

1.
   A. 100 liters
   B. 10 liters
   C. 1 liter

2.
   A. 100 milliliters
   B. 1 milliliter
   C. 1 liter

3.
   A. 1 liter
   B. 150 liters
   C. 15 milliliters

4.
   A. 5 milliliters
   B. 50 milliliters
   C. 500 milliliters

Write the two words that make each contraction.

5. she's _____

6. they're _____

7. aren't _____

8. you've _____

9. I've _____

10. I'd _____

11. it's _____

12. haven't _____

13. she'll _____

14. shouldn't _____

Reading Comprehension

Read the passage. Then, answer the questions.

Changing with the Seasons

We change the types of clothes we wear with the seasons to protect us from the weather. Animals change their appearance when seasons change to protect them from predators.

For example, the arctic fox has a thick, white fur coat in the winter. A white coat is not easy to see in the snow. This helps the fox hide. When spring comes, the fox's fur changes to brown or gray. It becomes the color of the ground.

The ptarmigan bird, or snow chicken, has white feathers in the winter. It, too, is hard to see in the snow. In the spring, the bird **molts**. This means that it sheds all of its feathers. The bird grows new feathers that are gray or brown and speckled. When the bird is very still, it looks like a rock.

15. What is the passage mostly about?

   A. how people change with the seasons

   B. how seasons change

   C. how animals change with the seasons

16. What color is the arctic fox's fur in the winter?

   A. brown   B. white   C. black   D. gray

17. What happens to the ptarmigan bird in the spring?

   A. It molts.   B. It flies south.

   C. Its feathers turn red.   D. It hides near rocks.

18. What does **molt** mean in the story?

   A. to change colors   B. to shed feathers

   C. to hide from an enemy   D. to run quickly

Division/Language Arts

Divide each set of objects into 3 equal groups. Then, divide to find each quotient.

1. 15 ÷ 3 = _____

2. 21 ÷ 3 = _____

3. 9 ÷ 3 = _____

Circle and write the correct contraction to complete each sentence.

4. __They've__ never played pickleball.

   They're   They'll   (They've)

5. _____ have a really fun time.

   We're   We'll   We've

6. _____ work as hard as I can.

   I'm   I've   I'll

7. _____ got to do it right the first time.

   We've   We'll   We're

8. _____ going to see a movie tonight.

   We'll   We're   We've

DAY 18

Reading Comprehension/Vocabulary

Read the story about Max and Julianna. Write *M* beside the phrases that describe Max and *J* beside the phrases that describe Julianna. Write *B* if the phrase describes both children.

Max and Julianna

Max and Julianna are twins. They have brown eyes and black hair. They are eight years old and go to school. Julianna likes math, and Max likes to read. They both like to play outside. Julianna likes to play basketball. Max likes to run and play tag. Julianna likes to ride her bike while Max walks their dog, Rover.

9. _____ has brown eyes
10. _____ likes to run
11. _____ is a twin
12. _____ likes to play basketball
13. _____ likes to read
14. _____ likes math
15. _____ is eight
16. _____ has a pet
17. _____ likes to ride bikes
18. _____ has black hair

Write the letter of the correct definition next to each vocabulary word.

19. _____ desert
20. _____ mountain
21. _____ valley
22. _____ ocean
23. _____ lake
24. _____ river

A. a tall piece of land
B. a flowing body of water
C. a body of water surrounded by land
D. low land between mountains or hills
E. a place that is very dry
F. a body of water that surrounds continents

Let's Play Today *See page 60.

Walk around either inside or outside doing lunges. Count how many lunge-steps you can take before stopping.

© Carson Dellosa Education

Language Arts

Important words in titles begin with capital letters. Look for the title in each sentence. Mark the letters that should be capitalized. Use this proofreading symbol: m.

1. Tyson's favorite book is *A year of billy miller*.

2. Have you ever seen the movie *matilda*?

3. When Dad was little, he loved to watch *schoolhouse rock*.

4. CJ knows all the words to his favorite song, "Don't worry, be happy."

5. Last weekend, we rented the movie *Against the wild*.

6. Grandma used to sing Cam to sleep by singing "walking after midnight."

To abbreviate a word means to shorten it. Draw a line to connect each word to its matching abbreviation.

7.	December	Dr.	8.	October	Rd.
	Doctor	oz.		foot	ft.
	Thursday	Dec.		Avenue	Ave.
	ounce	Thurs.		Road	Oct.

9.	yard	Wed.	10.	Senior	Sr.
	March	yd.		Monday	St.
	inch	in.		Fahrenheit	Mon.
	Wednesday	Mar.		Street	F

© Carson Dellosa Education

97

Grammar/Writing

Abstract nouns name feelings, concepts, and ideas. Some examples are *hope*, *bravery*, and *pride*. Underline the abstract noun in each sentence.

11. Mr. and Mrs. Ito were filled with pride when Mira won the spelling bee.

12. Grandma always talks about the wonderful childhood she had with her sisters.

13. My favorite thing about Jorge is his kindness.

14. Enzo could see the delight on Lea's face as she opened her gift.

15. "I really appreciate your honesty," said Principal Aziz.

16. I can count on Lynn to always tell me the truth.

Doors can lead to interesting places and things. Think of a door that could lead you to an interesting place. Describe the door and where it leads you. On a separate sheet of paper, draw a picture of your door.

_____

_____

_____

_____

_____

Geometry/Measurement

Skill IDs: 5H5 • PTF

DAY 20

Quadrilaterals are four-sided shapes. Draw an example of each quadrilateral named below. In the last box, draw a different quadrilateral.

1. square

2. rectangle

3. rhombus

4. other

Estimate the mass of each item. Circle your answer.

5.    A. 1 gram   B. 10 grams   C. 100 grams

6.    A. 2 kilograms   B. 200 kilograms   C. 25 kilograms

7.   A. 1 gram   B. 10 grams   C. 100 grams

8.    A. 1 kilogram   B. 100 kilograms   C. 10 kilograms

Fast Fun Fact

Your nose heats up when you lie.

© Carson Dellosa Education

99

DAY 20

Reading Comprehension

Read the poem. Then, answer the questions.

Two

Two living things, blowing in the wind.
One stands straight, the other bends.

One is a strong tree growing tall.
The other is grass ever so small.

Both are Mother Nature's gifts.
The tree you can climb. On the grass, you can sit.

Green is their color, brought on by the spring.
Grass or trees, they both make me sing!

9. What two things is the poem comparing?

   A. the grass and a tree

   B. a tree and a flower

   C. the wind and the rain

10. What does the line *Both are Mother Nature's gifts* mean?

_____

_____

11. Read each description. Decide if the words describe the grass, a tree, or both. Write an X in each correct column.

Alike or Different?	Grass	Tree
living thing		
stands straight in the wind		
bends in the wind		
tall		
small		
can be climbed		
can be sat on		
green in color		

Science Experiment

Paper Towel Preserver

Can you dunk a glass with a paper towel inside it into an aquarium filled with water and have the paper towel stay dry?

Materials:
- large, clear container or aquarium
- drinking glass (any size)
- dry paper towel
- water

Procedure:
With an adult, fill the aquarium with water.

Gently stuff the paper towel into the bottom of the glass. Turn the glass upside down to make sure that the paper towel does not fall out.

Keep the glass upside down. Slowly lower it straight down into the container of water until the paper towel and glass are both completely underwater. (Note: the experiment will not work if you tilt the glass at all.) Remove the glass from the water. Is the paper towel wet or dry?

What's This All About?
This experiment shows that air takes up space. As you lower the glass into the container of water, the air inside the glass displaces, or pushes away, the water in the container. Because the water is displaced, the paper towel stays dry.

More Fun Ideas to Try
If you are having a hard time seeing how air takes up space, put your hands on your chest. Inhale, hold your breath, and then exhale. Did you feel how air takes up space in your lungs?

Write About It
What is one thing you learned from this experiment that you would want to tell someone about? Write a sentence or two about it.

_____

_____

BONUS

Science Experiment

Air Friction

Which would drop faster if it fell from a two-story building: a penny or a sheet of paper? Which would hit the ground first? How does air affect falling objects?

Materials:
- sheet of paper
- penny
- a few small, unbreakable objects

Procedure:
Hold the penny and the sheet of paper in front of you and higher than your head. Let them both fall at the same time. Repeat this activity two more times.

Now, crumple the paper into a tight ball. Hold the paper and the penny in front of you and higher than your head. Let them both fall at the same time. Repeat this activity two more times.

Repeat the experiment with two sheets of paper that are crumpled, one loosely and one tightly. Then, try different coins and other objects. Which object falls the fastest?

What's This All About?
Even though we cannot see air, it has force. By crumpling the paper, you reduced the amount of force the air was able to put on the paper. We call this force *friction*.

Sometimes, it is good to have a lot of air friction. For example, a person using a parachute would want friction. The friction created by the parachute would slow their descent to Earth. Sometimes, it is good to have less air friction, such as when a pilot wants to make an airplane fly fast.

More Fun Ideas to Try:
- Make a simple parachute that uses air friction to slow a falling object. Use different materials (paper, fabrics, plastic bags) to make the parachute.

- With an adult, find pictures of different types of cars on the Internet. Look at their designs. Which cars do you think would cause less air friction?

Social Studies Activity

Locate It!

A grid (set of lines on a map) and coordinates (the letters and numbers beside the grid) help you locate places on a map. To find the mall on the map, look at section B,2. Use the map grid and map key to fill in the blanks with the coordinates for each place.

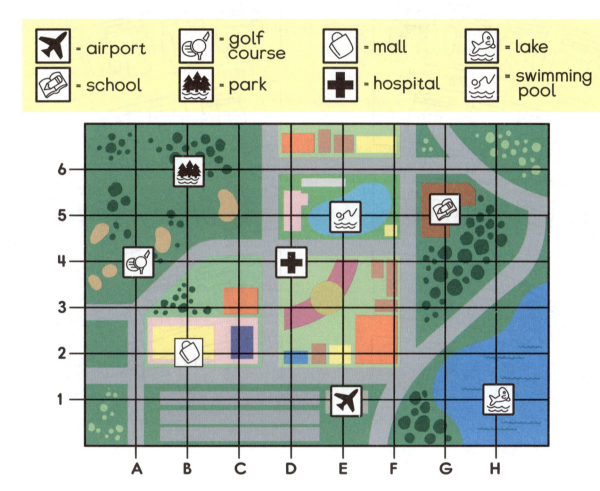

1. mall _____ B, 2 _____   2. lake _____

3. school _____   4. park _____

5. airport _____   6. hospital _____

7. golf course _____   8. swimming pool _____

© Carson Dellosa Education

103

BONUS

Social Studies Activity

Field Trip to a Broadway Play

Your class is going to a Broadway play. Follow the steps to find out where your friends are sitting at the play.

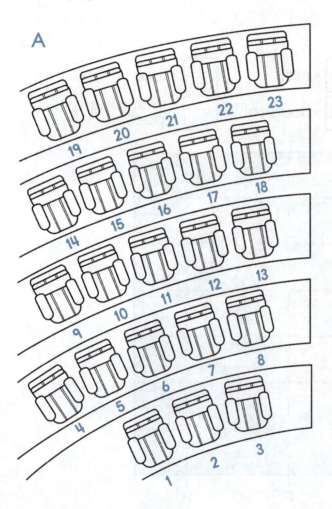
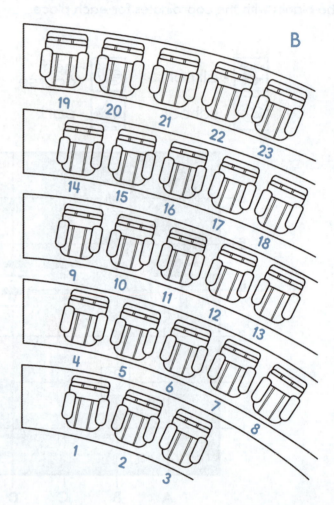

1. Emile is sitting in seat A, 11. Draw a red circle around Emile's seat.

2. Shauna is sitting in seat B, 9. Draw a blue square around Shauna's seat.

3. Diego is sitting in seat B, 5. Draw a green triangle around Diego's seat.

4. Phillip is sitting in seat A, 2. Color Phillip's seat orange.

5. Bo is sitting in seat A, 6. Color Bo's seat purple.

Social Studies Activity

Continent Scramble

A continent is the largest landmass on Earth. There are seven continents in the world. List the seven continents by unscrambling each name. Then, look at the map. Write the letter of each continent next to its name.

1. _____ ACIFRA _____

2. _____ THORN MICAERA _____

3. _____ EPRUEO _____

4. _____ HOUTS RECIMAA _____

5. _____ SAAI _____

6. _____ CTARNATCAI _____

7. _____ STRLAIAUA _____

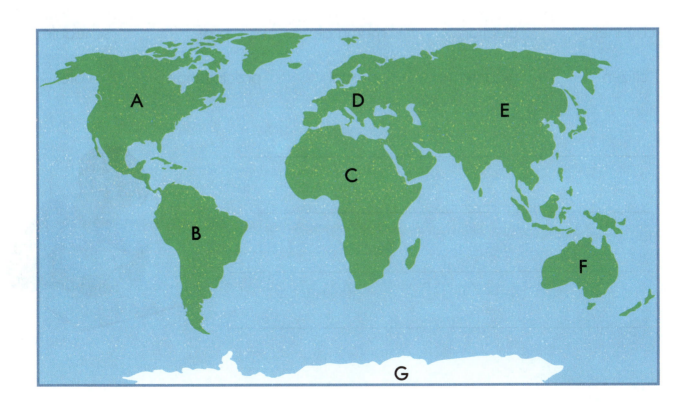

SECTION 3

Monthly Goals

Think of three goals to set for yourself this month. For example, you may want to learn five new math facts each week. Write your goals on the lines and review them with an adult.

Place a sticker next to each of your goals that you complete. Feel proud that you have met your goals!

1. _____ PLACE STICKER

2. _____ PLACE STICKER

3. _____ PLACE STICKER

Word List

The following words are used in this section. Read each word. Use a dictionary to look up each word that you do not know. Then, write two sentences. Use a word from the word list in each sentence.

| channel | election | mammal | pilot | schedule |
| citizen | gigantic | medal | precipitation | vote |

1. _____

2. _____

Introduction to Endurance

This section includes Let's Play Today and Mindful Moments activities that focus on endurance. These activities are designed to help you develop mental and physical stamina. If you have limited mobility, feel free to modify any suggested activity or choose a different one from the list on the following page.

Let's Play Today

Many children seem to have endless energy and can run, jump, and play for hours. But endurance does not come naturally to everyone. Developing endurance requires regular exercise that gets the body moving and the heart pumping, like arm punches, jumping jacks, dancing, and playing sports.

Make exercise a part of your everyday routine during the summer. Do things that make you breathe harder and move your body, such as playing hopscotch, going for a walk, kicking a ball with someone, climbing on playground equipment, riding a bike, and more.

Mindful Moments

Endurance means to stick with something, and it applies to the mind as well as to the body. If you have ever felt like giving up at something but instead you persevered and finished the task, you demonstrated endurance.

Think of a time when you wanted to quit a task. Maybe you didn't like the new game you were playing or the new skill you were practicing, and so you wanted to quit. What did you do? Realize that it often takes a while to learn something new. If you quit instead of persevering through a challenge, you wouldn't learn how to do new things and you wouldn't grow as a person. Endurance and perseverance build character and make people mentally strong. Quitting should be a last resort. Developing endurance at a young age will help you persevere through challenging physical and mental activities you encounter in life.

Engaging Online Practice

Bring learning to life with fun, interactive activities on IXL! Look for the Skill ID box and type the 3-digit code into the search bar on IXL.com or the IXL mobile app. Ten questions per day are free!

Skill IDs
5UN • D9K

© Carson Dellosa Education

SECTION 3

Let's Play Today

Get up and moving with these Let's Play Today activities. Section 3 focuses on endurance. Endurance is being able to complete many repetitions of a task, such as 10 jumping jacks, or perform an activity for an extended amount of time, such as riding a bike for 10 minutes. Building endurance will help you get through everyday tasks and find success with physical activities and sports. Use this list in addition to or as a replacement for any Let's Play Today suggestions on the activity pages. This list was developed to be inclusive of a variety of abilities. Choose the ones that are a good fit for you! Make modifications as needed. These activities may require adult supervision. See page 2 for full caution information.

Jump Rope:
Start by jumping rope for 30 seconds. Jump rope every day and try to increase the amount of time you can jump every day.

Freeze Dance:
Have one person control the music. Ask them to play a favorite song. Dance while the music plays. When the music pauses, stop dancing. If you dance after the music stops, the person controlling the music assigns an endurance challenge (5 jumping jacks, push-ups, etc.). Then you can rejoin the game.

Scavenger Hunt Hike:
Go on a scavenger hunt hike. Create a list of things you think you might see, such as a traffic light, a dog, or a particular type of flower. Cross items off your list as you go. You can also build endurance by going on a simple walk or run.

Fun on Wheels:
Go on a bike ride or play bike games. This works great with wheelchairs too. Create an obstacle course of cones and weave in and out, challenge a friend to a race, or use chalk to create roads, stop signs, and more.

Let's Go Team:
Playing team sports is a great way to build endurance. Basketball, soccer, football, softball, baseball, volleyball, and more are all great ways to improve endurance. Choose a favorite team sport and get a group of kids together to play at a local park.

108 © Carson Dellosa Education

Geometry/Grammar

Write one way in which the shapes in each pair are similar and different.

1. _____

2. _____

3. _____

4. _____

Underline the verb that completes each sentence.

5. Kylie and Kennise (are, is) going on a fall scavenger hunt.

6. Kylie (spot, spots) a pumpkin on a neighbor's porch.

7. Kennise (sees, see) a scarecrow.

8. The oak tree at the end of the street (drop, drops) acorns on the ground.

9. Busy squirrels (gather, gathers) the nuts.

 **Mindful Moment**

What makes you happy? Using paper and crayons or markers, draw a collage that includes all (or most of) the things that make you happy.

DAY 1

Reading Comprehension/Grammar

Read the stories. Circle what happens next.

10. Jeff put his arms around the box. He could not lift it. He would need some help. The box was too heavy for him.

    Jeff will _____ .

    A. run outside and play   B. ask his parent for help

    C. sit on the box   D. send the box to his friend

11. The children were playing outside. It started to get dark. They saw a flash of light and heard a loud sound. The wind began to blow.

    "Let's go," shouted Malik. "It's _____ ."

    A. time to eat   B. going to blow us away

    C. going to rain soon   D. time for bed

Choose a conjunction from the box to complete each sentence. Do not use the same conjunction more than once.

| and | although | while | but | or | whether |

12. _____ Mom doesn't like coffee, she loves the way it smells.

13. Kali took out the garbage, _____ Maria washed the dishes.

14. _____ the sun comes out or not, we will enjoy the party.

15. Mickey is almost a year old, _____ he is not walking yet.

110 © Carson Dellosa Education

Measurement/Vocabulary  DAY 2

Michi is helping her grandpa build a chicken coop. Her grandpa asked her to measure the lengths of the boards in the garage. Draw an X on the line plot to show the measurement of each board.

Board A	$38\frac{1}{2}$ inches
Board B	$40\frac{3}{4}$ inches
Board C	$38\frac{1}{2}$ inches
Board D	$41\frac{1}{4}$ inches
Board E	$38\frac{1}{2}$ inches
Board F	$40\frac{3}{4}$ inches

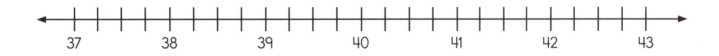

Add the ending shown to each base word to make a new word. Don't forget to change the spelling of the base word when the ending is added.

change *y* to *i*

1. try + es = _____

2. happy + ness = _____

double the final consonant

3. sit + ing = _____

4. hop + ed = _____

drop the final *e*

5. smile + ed = _____

6. slide + ing = _____

change *ie* to *y* or *y* to *ie*

7. lie + ing = _____

8. puppy + s = _____

© Carson Dellosa Education   111

DAY 2 — Measurement/Writing

Skill ID 5HA — Search for this skill ID on IXL.com for more practice!

To find the area of a rectangle, multiply its length by its width. Solve each problem.

9. Tamika wants to buy a rug that is 5 feet wide by 7 feet long. What area will the rug cover?

   _____ square feet

10. Jalen's backyard pool is 16 feet long by 10 feet wide. What is the area of the pool?

    _____ square feet

11. Kyra got a tumbling mat for her birthday. It is 12 feet long by 6 feet wide. What is the area of the mat?

    _____ square feet

12. Mr. O'Malley has to replace part of his garage roof. The damaged spot measures 5 feet wide by 3 feet long. What is its area?

    _____ square feet

Imagine that you are collecting items for a time capsule that will be opened in 20 years. What things would you put in the capsule to tell about your life right now?

_____

_____

_____

_____

Addition & Subtraction/Grammar

Skill IDs: 2TD • RQ5

DAY 3

Add or subtract to solve each problem.

1. 240
   +125

2. 346
   +231

3. 115
   +460

4. 219
   +674

5. 532
   +164

6. 756
   −110

7. 875
   −241

8. 679
   −336

9. 572
   −320

10. 348
   −123

11. 435
   +281

12. 568
   +272

13. 626
   +193

14. 271
   +378

15. 492
   +247

Write *N* if the verb is in the present tense (happening now). Write *P* if the verb is in the past tense (already happened). Write *F* if the verb is in the future tense (will happen in the future).

16. _____ We will eat later.

17. _____ I have a sandwich.

18. _____ Grant ate a pickle.

19. _____ We will go home soon.

20. _____ I love pickles!

21. _____ Naomi is having a party.

22. _____ I swam with my friends.

23. _____ Jaydon cleaned his room.

Let's Play Today *See page 108.

Find a set of stairs in your home or outside. Run up and down them as many times as you can. Count them as you go.

© Carson Dellosa Education

113

Reading Comprehension

Read the TV schedule. Then, answer the questions.

Channel	7:00	7:30	8:00	8:30	9:00	9:30	10:00	10:30
2	Quiz Game Show	Jump Start			Summer the Dog		News	
4	Lucky Guess	You Should Know	Wednesday Night at the Movies Friends Forever				News	
5	Best Friends	Mary's Secret	Where They Are	Time to Hope	Raven's Talk Show		News	
7	123 Oak Street	Lost Alone	One More Time	Sports			News	
11	Your Health	Eating Right	Food News		Cooking With Carson		Home Decor	Shop Now
24	Silly Rabbit	Clyde the Clown	Ball o' Fun	Slime and Rhyme	Cartoon Alley		Fun Times	Make Me Laugh

24. What does this schedule show?

   A. times and channels of TV shows

   B. times and channels of radio programs

   C. the number of people who like different shows

25. On which channels is the news on at 10:00?

   A. 2, 5, and 11   B. 3, 4, and 11   C. 2, 4, 5, and 7

26. What time does the show *Silly Rabbit* begin?

   A. 7:00   B. 7:30   C. 8:30

Geometry/Language Arts

DAY 4

Follow the directions.

1. Draw lines to divide the square into 4 equal parts. Write numbers in the boxes to make a fraction that names one part.

2. Draw lines to divide the rectangle into 6 equal parts. Write numbers in the boxes to make a fraction that names one part.

3. Draw lines to divide the circle into 3 equal parts. Write numbers in the boxes to make a fraction that names one part.

 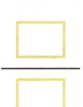

Change each declarative sentence into an interrogative sentence.

4. The busy mail carrier is leaving. _____Is the busy mail carrier leaving?_____

5. That man is Felix's neighbor. _____

6. She can ride her new bike. _____

7. I will ride the black horse. _____

© Carson Dellosa Education

115

In a dictionary, guide words are at the top of each page. The guide word on the left tells the first word on the page. The guide word on the right tells the last word on the page. Circle the word that would be on the page with each set of guide words.

8.	patter – penguin	panda	pit	paw
9.	match – monkey	math	magic	motor
10.	bear – buffalo	bunny	bat	bison
11.	hammer – happy	hall	hand	hair
12.	rabbit – rack	race	racket	radio

13. In the table, color the words with *soft c* blue. Color the words with *soft g* orange.

page	space	mice	large	rage
cage	dance	bounce	ginger	gentle
lace	fence	bridge	judge	cent
cell	age	germ	giraffe	face

Geometry and Measurement/Language Arts

Write a multiplication problem to find the area of each rectangle.

1.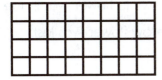

   Area = _____ × _____ = _____ square units

2.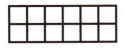

   Area = _____ × _____ = _____ square units

3.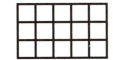

   Area = _____ × _____ = _____ square units

4.

   Area = _____ × _____ = _____ square units

Write *E* for each exclamatory sentence. Write *D* for each declarative sentence. Write *I* for each interrogative sentence.

5. _____ What did they say?

6. _____ I am so happy for you!

7. _____ It's a boy!

8. _____ The card is green.

Write each exclamatory sentence with a capital letter and an exclamation point (!).

9. watch out _____

10. i had a great day _____

Reading Comprehension/Grammar

Read the story. Then, complete the picture to match the story.

Margaret planted five flowers in pots. She put the flowers in a row. The white flower was in the middle. The purple flower was second. The orange flower was not first. The yellow flower was last.

Write the missing comparative adjectives.

11. _____fast_____   _____   _____

12. _____   _____   _____tallest_____

13. _____   _____colder_____   _____

14. _____bright_____   _____   _____brightest_____

15. _____   _____deeper_____   _____

Fast Fun Fact

Alaska is just two miles away from Russia!

Multiplication/Language Arts

Multiply to find each product. Then, draw a line to match each set to the correct multiplication problem.

1. 4 × 3 = __12__

2. 3 × 3 = _____

3. 5 × 2 = _____

4. 3 × 2 = _____

5. 2 × 4 = _____

Write *IM* for each imperative sentence. Write *D* for each declarative sentence. Write *I* for each interrogative sentence. Write *E* for each exclamatory sentence.

6. _____ Make a card for Nana.

7. _____ Use markers.

8. _____ She will love it!

9. _____ Show your grandma.

10. _____ Tell her how you made it.

11. _____ Cards are great gifts.

12. _____ Has your grandpa seen it?

13. _____ The card looks great!

© Carson Dellosa Education

119

DAY 6

Search for this skill ID on IXL.com for more practice!

Reading Comprehension

Read the story. Then, answer the questions.

The Giant Cookie

My dad baked a giant cookie for me. I sat on my front steps to eat it. But, before I could take a bite, my friend Ivy came by.

"Will you share your cookie with me?" Ivy asked. I broke my cookie into two pieces: one for me and one for Ivy. But, before we could each take a bite, Jermaine and Drew came by.

"Will you share your cookie with us?" they asked. Ivy and I each broke our cookie into two pieces. Now, we had four pieces: one for me, one for Ivy, one for Jermaine, and one for Drew. But, before we could each take a bite, four more friends came by.

"Will you share your cookie with us?" they asked. Ivy, Jermaine, Drew, and I all broke our pieces in half. Now, we had enough to share between eight friends. I looked at my giant cookie. It was not a giant cookie anymore.

"Hey, does anyone know what is gigantic when there's one but small when there are eight?" I asked.

"No, what?" my friends asked.

"My cookie!" I laughed.

14. What happened to the cookie?

　A. It was shared between friends.　　**B.** It was lost.

　C. It was burned.　　**D.** It was dropped on the floor.

15. Number the events from the story in order.

　_____ Jermaine and Drew came by.　　_____ Ivy came by.

　_____ Dad baked a cookie.　　_____ Four friends came by.

Mindful Moment

On a smooth surface like a table, slowly trace and retrace your index finger in a figure-8 shape for one minute. As you do this, repeat a positive thought about yourself, such as "I am a good friend."

© Carson Dellosa Education

Multiplication/Language Arts

DAY 7

Multiply to find each product.

1. 5 × 1 = _____
2. 5 × 5 = _____
3. 3 × 4 = _____

4. 1 × 0 = _____
5. 2 × 2 = _____
6. 4 × 5 = _____

7. 3 × 5 = _____
8. 1 × 1 = _____
9. 2 × 5 = _____

10. 7
    × 1
    ___

11. 4
    × 2
    ___

12. 2
    × 3
    ___

13. 3
    × 3
    ___

14. 4
    × 0
    ___

Write two exclamatory sentences and two declarative sentences. Use a word from the word bank in each sentence.

| attention | calmly | famous | free | million |
| moment | rain | shiver | station | strange |

15. _____

16. _____

17. _____

18. _____

© Carson Dellosa Education

121

Use the dictionary entry to answer the questions.

> **germ** \'jerm\ n **1.** disease-producing microbe **2.** a bud or seed

19. What part of speech is *germ*? _____

20. Which definition of *germ* deals with growing plants? _____

21. Would *germinate* come before or after *germ* in the dictionary? _____

22. Use *germ* in a sentence. _____

_____

Write a title for each list.

23. _____

robin

wren

blue jay

canary

24. _____

paper

glue

scissors

crayons

25. _____

lion

tiger

bear

elephant

26. _____

milk

tea

water

juice

Multiplication/Grammar

Solve each problem.

1. Maddie has 3 vases with 4 flowers in each vase. How many total flowers does she have?

   _____ × _____ = _____ flowers

2. Mario has 4 packs of gum. There are 5 pieces in each pack. How many pieces of gum does he have?

   _____ × _____ = _____ pieces

3. Jawan has 3 glasses. He put 2 straws in each glass. How many straws did Jawan put in the glasses?

   _____ × _____ = _____ straws

4. We have 4 tables for the party. Each table needs 4 chairs. How many total chairs do we need?

   _____ × _____ = _____ chairs

Underline the pronoun that completes each sentence.

5. Caleb borrowed six books from the library, but he has lost one of (it, them).

6. At the fair, several kids lost (them, their) balloons.

7. Taj has three frogs as pets and loves (their, them) very much.

8. Liam remembered to brush (their, his) teeth before school.

9. The hurricane made landfall at 6:00, and (it, them) is headed this way!

10. Each of the girls gets an apple for (her, his) snack.

Search for this skill ID on IXL.com for more practice!

Reading Comprehension/Writing

Read the paragraph. Then, answer the questions.

Malia's Day

Malia got up late today, so she missed the bus. Her aunt had to walk Malia to school. She was tired and cranky when she got there. She promised herself that she would never sleep late again.

11. Why did Malia miss the bus? _____

12. Why did she have to walk? _____
    _____

13. What advice do you have for Malia? _____
    _____

Imagine you find a treasure map and a letter in your mailbox. Start a story about it below. Who sent the letter? If you look for the treasure, do you find it? If you find it, what is it? Finish your story on another piece of paper.

_____
_____
_____
_____

Let's Play Today *See page 108.

Do push-ups on the floor or against a wall for 30 seconds.

124 © Carson Dellosa Education

Division/Language Arts

Divide each set of objects into 2 equal groups. Then, divide to find each quotient.

1.

   6 ÷ 2 = _____

2.

   4 ÷ 2 = _____

3.

   10 ÷ 2 = _____

4.

   8 ÷ 2 = _____

A simple sentence has one subject and one verb. A compound sentence is two simple sentences joined with a conjunction like and. A complex sentence is a simple sentence combined with a group of words called a clause.

Write *S* for each simple sentence, *C* for each compound sentence, and *CX* for each complex sentence.

5. _____ The hummingbird drank from a flower, and then it flew away.

6. _____ Juan went to the park on Saturday.

7. _____ Because Lucia has a beautiful voice, she's going to take singing lessons this fall.

8. _____ Sarah plays basketball every day.

9. _____ Although the temperature dropped last night, the plants were okay.

Read the paragraph. Then, follow the directions.

Laiana's Summer

Laiana is very busy in the summer. She likes to sleep until eight o'clock in the morning. After she gets up, she helps her father work in the garden. Laiana reads and plays with her friends every day. She also likes to swim and play soccer with her brothers. Most of all, she likes to ride her bike.

10. Underline the topic sentence.

11. What time does Laiana get up? _____

12. How does Laiana help her father? _____

13. Write three other things that Laiana likes to do in the summer. _____

_____

Underline an adverb to complete each sentence.

14. Our puppy plays (more joyfully, joyfuller) with children than anyone else.

15. Joseph arrived (latest, most late) at the theater.

16. Please try to whisper (softer, more softly) while the baby sleeps.

17. Eli jumped (most farthest, farthest) of anyone in the competition.

18. The stars seem to shine (brightliest, most brightly) far from the city.

Fractions/Language Arts

Compare the fractions shown by the colored areas in each pair of circles. Use the greater than (>), less than (<), or equal to (=) symbols.

1.
2.
3.
4.
5.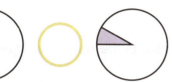
6.

Capitalize the first, last, and all important words in a story or book title. Write each story title correctly.

7. an exciting camping trip   An Exciting Camping Trip
8. my ride on a donkey _____
9. the day I missed school _____
10. fun, fabulous pets _____
11. a fire drill _____
12. my summer job _____

Fast Fun Fact

Crabs have their taste buds on their feet.

© Carson Dellosa Education

127

DAY 10 — Multiplication/Vocabulary

Numbers can be multiplied in different ways to get the same product. Write a product on each line.

13. (2 × 3) × 4 = 24

    6 × 4 = _____

14. 3 × 6 = 18

    6 × 3 = _____

15. (3 × 4) + (3 × 2) = 18

    3 × (4 + 2) = _____

16. 15 × 2 = 30

    2 × 15 = _____

Similar words can have different shades of meaning. Write each word in the sentence where it makes the most sense.

17. happy, overjoyed

    Sonya was _____ to see her grandparents for the first time in nearly ten years.

    Lucas was _____ that he could sleep in on Saturday morning.

18. cross, furious

    Miguel felt _____ when he couldn't find his football helmet.

    Mrs. Hitch was _____ that the babysitter forgot to pick up the kids at school.

19. gigantic, large

    A _____ moth fluttered around the porch light.

    During the hurricane, several _____ waves nearly destroyed the village.

Division/Reading Comprehension

DAY 11

Divide to find each quotient.

1. 6)̄36
2. 7)̄42
3. 8)̄56
4. 5)̄45

5. 3)̄21
6. 9)̄63
7. 4)̄36
8. 6)̄54

Circle each word that should have a capital letter. Then, answer the questions about the story.

Our Camping Trip

mom, dad, and i went camping last week. We went with Uncle louis and Aunt greta. We had fun. Dad and uncle louis climbed on rocks. Aunt greta and I saw a chipmunk. We all hiked on exciting trails. There was only one problem. mom, dad, and i did not bring sweaters. Dad said that it would be warm in the desert. He was wrong. At night, it was very cold. uncle Louis and aunt greta had sweaters. Mom, dad, and I stayed close to the fire. Next time, we will bring warmer clothes.

9. What was Dad wrong about? _____

10. Who tells the story? _____

11. How do Mom, Dad, and the author solve their problem? _____

© Carson Dellosa Education

129

DAY 11

Language Arts/Multiplication & Division

Read each sentence. Then, circle whether each sentence is reality or fantasy.

12. A beaver is a mammal that builds dams.   reality   fantasy

13. The fairy lived inside a mushroom.   reality   fantasy

14. People can build brick walls.   reality   fantasy

15. The dog sang a song.   reality   fantasy

Write a number in the star to complete each equation.

16. 8 × ☆ = 56   17. ☆ ÷ 9 = 2   18. 7 × 4 = ☆

19. ☆ × 10 = 90   20. 40 ÷ ☆ = 8

21. 5 × ☆ = 35   22. ☆ × 3 = 21   23. 20 ÷ 4 = ☆

Mindful Moment

Use all 5 senses to name 5 different things you can see, hear, smell, touch, and taste.

Fractions/Language Arts  DAY 12

The fraction $\frac{3}{1}$ is the same as the whole number 3. Write numbers in the boxes to make a fraction that shows each whole number.

1. 5

2. 11

3. 24

4. 9

Answer the questions.

5. How many fourths make one whole? _____

6. How many eighths make one whole? _____

7. How many twelfths make one whole? _____

8. How many fifths make one whole? _____

Add commas and quotation marks where they are needed. Use this symbol to add a ⁀ comma and this symbol to add quotation marks ⁀.

9. "Did you know that Reid lives in Dallas, Texas?

10. "Mr. Jarvis is my neighbor said Grandma.

11. Is Nasir's birthday in April?" asked Sasha.

12. "My mother and I shop at Smith's Market" I added.

Read the passage. Then, answer the questions.

Amelia Earhart

Amelia Earhart was a famous airplane pilot. She was born in 1897. She saw her first airplane at the Iowa State Fair at age 10. Amelia Earhart started taking flying lessons in 1921. Then, she bought her first plane. She named the plane *Canary* because it was bright yellow.

In 1932, Amelia Earhart became the first woman to fly alone across the Atlantic Ocean. The United States Congress gave her a medal called the Distinguished Flying Cross after this accomplishment. Amelia Earhart set many new flying records. Also in 1932, she became the first woman to fly alone nonstop from one coast of the United States to another. In 1937, she decided to fly around the world. Her plane was lost over the Pacific Ocean. Amelia Earhart was never heard from again.

13. What is the main idea of this passage?

   A. Amelia Earhart flew around the world.

   B. Amelia Earhart was a famous pilot who set many flying records.

   C. Amelia Earhart had a yellow airplane called *Canary*.

14. How does the author order or organize the information in this passage? _____
_____

15. Why did Earhart call her first airplane *Canary*? _____

16. Why did Earhart receive a medal? _____
_____

17. What happened to Earhart in 1937? _____
_____

Language Arts

The phrase "It's raining cats and dogs" doesn't really mean that animals are falling from the sky! It is an expression, or an idiom. Write a sentence for each idiom.

1. I'm all ears
   _____

2. green thumb
   _____

3. get the ball rolling
   _____

4. hit the hay
   _____

Unscramble and rewrite each sentence correctly. Add capital letters, periods, or question marks where they are needed.

5. birds do live where _____

6. very my hard works sister _____

7. swim can like fish a she _____

8. green grass why is _____

Let's Play Today *See page 108.

Lay a few items, like shoes or pillows, on the floor or ground to create an obstacle course. Jump from one object to the next, landing next to each object.

Reading Comprehension

Read the story. Then, circle the letter of the best summary.

Water Fun

Zayne loved to play in the water. Every time it rained, he would run outside to play in the puddles. His dog splashed in the water with him. Zayne splashed water on anyone who came near. Soon, his friends would not play with him because he always got them wet. One day, a big truck went by and splashed water all over Zayne. He got so wet that he decided not to splash people anymore.

9. **A.** Zayne liked to play in puddles of water. He got wet. He did not splash anymore after that.

   B. Zayne liked to play in puddles of water. He splashed water on people. One day, a truck splashed him. He stopped splashing others.

A book's title usually gives you an idea of what the book will be about. Match each book title to the contents of the book. Write the letter on the line.

10. _____ Taking Care of Plants   **A.** a mystery about a plant

11. _____ My Sloth Ate My Homework   **B.** a biography about a pilot

12. _____ Frida Kahlo: My Life as an Artist   **C.** a how-to book about plants

13. _____ The Missing Cactus   **D.** a science fiction book about bugs

14. _____ The Bugs That Took Over the World   **E.** a funny book about a pet

15. _____ Amelia Earhart: Woman Aviator **F.** an autobiography about an artist

16. _____ The Life of a Sloth   **G.** a nonfiction book about an animal

17. _____ Soups, Salads, and Sandwiches **H.** a cookbook

Fractions/Language Arts

Mark each fraction on the number line beside it.

1. 1/2

   3/6

2. 2/3

   4/6

3. What do you notice about the fraction in each pair? _____

Add a simple sentence after each conjunction below to form a compound sentence.

4. Mr. Sanchez is a teacher, but

   Mr. Sanchez is a teacher, but he doesn't work at my school.

5. Mom is teaching Omar how to mow the lawn, but

   _____

6. Hannah feeds the cats each morning, or

   _____

7. It is supposed to snow on Tuesday, so

   _____

8. Beatrix just joined the swim team, and

   _____

Search for this skill ID on IXL.com for more practice!

Language Arts/Writing

Look at the index from a book about flowers. Then, write the page number where you would find the information on each flower.

9. tulip _____

10. pansy _____

11. daisy _____

12. rose _____

13. zinnia _____

14. lily _____

A	G	R
allium............45	gardens............2	rose...............21
aster..............62	gladiolus...........7	**S**
B	**I**	stamen..........6, 7
blossoms..........13	iris..................8	stigma...........6, 7
buttercup........65	**L**	**T**
C	larkspur...........47	thistle..............27
cowslip............25	lily.................42	tulip................26
D	**M**	**W**
daffodil...........27	marigold..........29	wisteria............20
dahlia.............19	**P**	**Z**
daisy..............15	pansy..............31	zinnia.............60
	petals..............6	

Write a paragraph about something that you like to do or learn about, such as baking, playing an instrument, or reading about dinosaurs.

_____
_____
_____
_____
_____
_____
_____

Fractions/Language Arts

Draw a line to match the shapes in each group that show the same fraction shaded.

1. 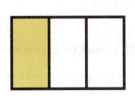 2.

Write the meaning of each underlined idiom.

3. Mrs. Wen has her hands full with the twins, who are two years old.

_____

4. After the storm, the flat tire, and Henry's tantrum, Dad was ready to call it a day and head home.

_____

5. I'm going to have to hit the books tonight if I want to be ready for the test.

_____

6. On accident, Olivia spilled the beans about the surprise party.

_____

7. Destiny is a night owl, but everyone else in her family goes to bed early.

_____

Reading Comprehension

Read the passage. Then, answer the questions.

The Right to Vote

Voting in government elections is very important. In the United States and Canada, a person must be a citizen of the country and be at least 18 years old to vote in an election. Not everyone could vote in the past. In the United States, no women were allowed to vote until 1920. A law was passed in 1965 that protected the rights of adults of all races to vote. When a person votes, they help decide who will serve in the government and what kinds of laws will be passed. Some people say that voting is the most important thing that people can do as citizens.

8. What is the main idea of this passage?

   A. A person must be at least 18 years old to vote in an election.

   B. Not everyone can vote in the United States.

   C. Voting is an important thing for people to be able to do.

9. Who can vote in the United States and Canada? _____

10. When were women in the United States first allowed to vote? _____

11. What happened in the United States after a law was passed in 1965?

   _____

12. Why is voting important? _____

   _____

Fast Fun Fact
Astronauts can vote in elections from outer space.

138 © Carson Dellosa Education

Fractions/Language Arts

Color the objects to show each fraction.

1. Color one-third.

   $\frac{1}{3}$

2. Color two-fourths.

   $\frac{2}{4}$

   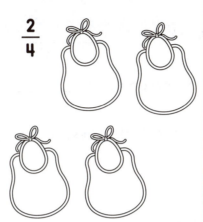

3. Color three-sixths.

   $\frac{3}{6}$

4. Color one-sixth.

   $\frac{1}{6}$

   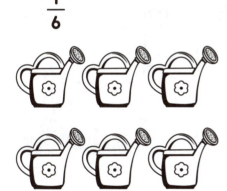

5. Color one-fourth.

   $\frac{1}{4}$

   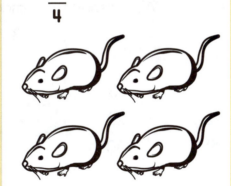

6. Color five-eighths.

   $\frac{5}{8}$

Add commas where they are needed in the paragraph.

Land Formations and Bodies of Water

The Earth has many mountains, rivers, lakes oceans and continents. The Andes the Rockies and the Urals are mountain ranges. The Amazon the Nile and the Hudson are rivers. Lake Erie Lake Ontario and Lake Huron are three of the Great Lakes. The Pacific the Atlantic and the Arctic are oceans. Europe, Asia and Africa are continents. New Zealand Greenland and Iceland are islands.

DAY 16

Language Arts/Time

Write the name of the person who is talking in each sentence.

7. Travis said, "Trent, you need to go to bed." _____

8. "Is this your book, Lamar?" asked Keisha. _____

9. Lamar replied, "No, Keisha, it is not my book." _____

10. "Will you take the dog for a walk, Mia?" asked Mrs. Travers. _____

Use the calendar to answer the questions.

August						
Sunday	Monday	Tuesday	Wednesday	Thursday	Friday	Saturday
		1	2	3	4	5
6	7	8	9	10	11	12
13	14	15	16	17	18	19
20	21	22	23	24	25	26
27	28	29	30	31		

11. What day of the week is August 18? _____

12. How many Wednesdays are in August? _____

13. What is the date of the last Saturday in August? _____

14. What day of the week will September 1 be? _____

Mindful Moment

Take a nature walk with an adult near your home. Notice everything that flies, walks, crawls, or swims.

Writing/Language Arts

Do you wish you had a later bedtime? Write a persuasive paragraph explaining your opinion. Include good reasons to support your opinion.

_____

_____

_____

_____

Rewrite each sentence correctly. Add capital letters, periods, and question marks where they are needed.

1. bobby has a dog named shadow

   _____

2. do bluebirds eat insects

   _____

3. can i borrow your video game

   _____

4. my name is nikki

   _____

Language Arts

An analogy compares two pairs of items based on a similar relationship between the items. Write the correct word from the word bank to complete each analogy.

| cat | ground | window | ~~water~~ | trees | cow |

5. Car is to road as boat is to __water__.

6. Bird is to sky as worm is to _____.

7. City is to buildings as forest is to _____.

8. Knob is to door as pane is to _____.

9. Cub is to bear as calf is to _____.

10. Quack is to duck as meow is to _____.

Choose an adjective or adverb from the box to complete each sentence. Write it on the line.

| tightly | red | slowly | heavy |

11. The girl walked _____ home from school.

12. She was wearing _____ pants.

13. She dropped her _____ backpack by the door.

14. Her grandma _____ hugged her.

Graphing/Language Arts

The bar graph shows concession stand sales at a baseball game. Use the bar graph to answer the questions.

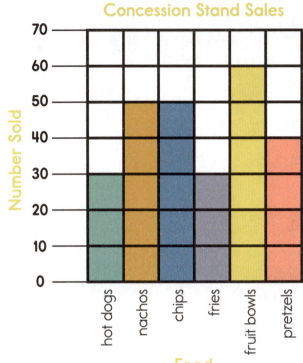

1. Which two items had the fewest sales?

   _____

2. Which item had the most sales?

   _____

3. How many more nachos were sold than hot dogs?

   _____

4. How many more chips were sold than pretzels?

   _____

Write three sentences. Use a word from the word bank in each sentence. Use capital letters, periods, question marks, and exclamation points where they are needed.

adult	during	finish	interested
job	prepare	summer	work

5. _____

6. _____

7. _____

DAY 18 — Fractions/Writing

Draw a line between fractions that are equivalent, or equal.

8. $\frac{1}{2}$  $\frac{3}{9}$

9. $\frac{4}{6}$  $\frac{2}{4}$

10. $\frac{4}{4}$ $\frac{2}{3}$

11. $\frac{1}{3}$ $\frac{1}{1}$

Imagine that you saw a dinosaur walking down your street. What did the dinosaur look like? What would happen next? Write the beginning of your story here. Finish it on another piece of paper.

_____

_____

_____

Let's Play Today *See page 108.

On a soft surface like carpet or a yoga mat, do 10 somersaults.

Graphing/Writing

The line graph shows precipitation changes during a year in Chicago, Illinois. Use the line graph to answer the questions.

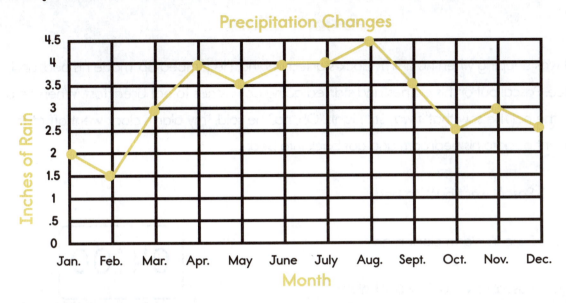

1. Which three months received the same amount of rain?

   _____

2. What was the most rainfall received in one month? _____

3. Which month received the least amount of precipitation? _____

Use a dictionary to look up the word *consequence*. Why should you think about consequences of actions?

_____

_____

_____

Reading Comprehension/Writing

Read the story. Number the events in the order that they happened.

The Alarm Clock

Pascal was sleeping when his alarm clock started ringing. He jumped up, made his bed, and washed his face. Pascal put on his clothes and started going downstairs to eat breakfast. When he passed the window in the hall, he saw that it was still night. "Oh, no," he said, "my alarm clock went off at the wrong time!" Pascal went back to his bedroom and got back into bed.

4. _____ Pascal went back to bed.

5. _____ Pascal's alarm clock rang.

6. _____ Pascal saw that it was still night.

7. _____ Pascal made his bed and washed his face.

8. _____ Pascal started going downstairs to eat breakfast.

What would your day be like if you woke up one day as an adult? Start your story here and use another piece of paper to finish it.

_____

_____

_____

_____

_____

Graphing/Grammar

Use the pictograph to answer the questions.

Number of Flowers Picked
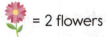 = 2 flowers

J'Nai	🌸🌸🌸	Beth	🌸🌸🌸🌸🌸
Sue	🌸🌸🌸🌸🌸	Lori	🌸🌸🌸🌸
Dante	🌸🌸	Jamal	🌸🌸🌸

1. How many flowers does 🌸 stand for? _____

2. How many total flowers did Sue and J'Nai pick? _____

3. Who picked the most flowers? _____

4. Which children picked the same number of flowers? _____

5. Who picked the fewest flowers? _____

Write the part of speech for each underlined word. Write your answer above the word.

Vegetables

Do you like vegetables? I like some vegetables. I do not like others. I like snow peas. They taste best fresh from the garden. They are green and sweet. I like fresh, crunchy carrots, too. I pick them from the garden. I love corn on the cob. I pull off the husks. Mom boils the corn. I eat the yellow corn from one end to the other.

DAY 20

Search for this skill ID on IXL.com for more practice!

Reading Comprehension

Read the story. Then, answer the questions.

Ready for the Play-Off

Austin was too excited about the baseball play-off game to think about the model volcano he and Pablo were building in science class.

"Do you want to tear the paper into strips or dip them in paste and put them on?" Pablo asked Austin.

"Home run!" said Austin.

Pablo looked puzzled. Austin's face burned with embarrassment. "I'm sorry. I was thinking about the game."

Pablo laughed. "Oh!" he said. "Well, that explains it. Do you think we'll win?"

"My big brother says that Ms. Lee's class hasn't won a play-off game in at least five years. Maybe we'll be the first," Austin said.

Austin saw Ms. Lee walking toward them. He picked up a piece of newspaper and tore it into strips. Pablo understood. He dipped a strip into the paste and smoothed it onto the side of the model volcano.

"You boys should start cleaning up now," Ms. Lee said. "We don't want to be late." Austin and Pablo carried their model to the science table and cleaned up. They were back in their seats and ready to go in five minutes.

6. Who is the main character in the story?

   A. Austin's brother   B. Austin   C. Ms. Lee

7. What does the main character want to do? _____

8. Where does the story take place?

   A. in a classroom   B. in a gym   C. on the baseball field

Fast Fun Fact

There are volcanoes in outer space. The largest volcano in our solar system is on Mars!

148   © Carson Dellosa Education

Science Experiment

An Oily Separation

How can a mixture of oil and water be separated?

Materials:
- 16-ounce clear drinking glass
- spoon
- eyedropper
- 6.75 ounces (200 mL) of water
- 6.75 ounces (200 mL) of vegetable oil
- clear glass measuring cup

Procedure:
Pour the water into the drinking glass. Add the vegetable oil to the water. Stir the water and oil with the spoon and observe. Then, let the water and oil sit for 10–15 minutes.

Use the eyedropper to pull the oil from the top of the water and place it into the measuring cup. Record the amount, or volume, of oil collected. Then, subtract that amount from the amount of oil that was first added to the drinking glass. Record your results. Do the experiment two more times. Record your data in the table.

Trial	Initial Volume of Oil	Volume of Oil Collected	Difference
1			
2			
3			

What happens when you stir the water and the oil? _____

_____

What happens when you stop stirring the water and the oil? _____

_____

What's This All About?
Sometimes, liquids separate into layers. Oil and water separate into layers. Water is heavier than oil, so it sinks to the bottom of a container.

Think About It
- What is an eyedropper used for? Why do you need one for this experiment?
- What causes and effects can be seen in this experiment?

Bonus — Science Experiment

Disappearing Act

Water can disappear by evaporating. Sometimes, water leaves things behind when it evaporates.

Materials:
- masking tape
- 2 pie tins
- drinking glass
- 1 tablespoon of salt
- measuring cup
- pencil
- warm water
- spoon

Procedure:
Use the masking tape and a pencil to label the outside of the pie tins. Label one *salt water* and the other *tap water*.

Use the measuring cup to pour 4 ounces (118.29 mL) of warm water into a drinking glass. Add one tablespoon of salt to the water. Use the spoon to stir the water until the salt dissolves. Add salt until no more will dissolve. This is called a saturated solution. Pour the saturated solution into the pie tin labeled salt water.

Use the measuring cup to pour 4 ounces (118.29 mL) of tap water into the pie tin labeled tap water. Put the pie tins side-by-side in a safe place. Record your observations each day until the water in both pie tins has evaporated.

What's This All About?
This activity uses salt water as the basis for crystal formation. The water evaporates from the pan. Salt, a mineral, is left behind.

More Fun Ideas to Try:
- Change the amount of salt in the water. Find out if it affects how quickly the water evaporates.
- With an adult, change the liquid you use. Try vinegar, lemonade, etc. Use the same amount of salt and change the amount of liquid.

© Carson Dellosa Education

Social Studies Activity

Land Features

Write the letter of each landform next to its name.

1. _____ lake
2. _____ valley
3. _____ river
4. _____ peninsula
5. _____ volcano
6. _____ island
7. _____ mountain
8. _____ ocean
9. _____ savanna

BONUS — Search for this skill ID on IXL.com for more practice!

Social Studies Activity

Countries and Cities

Political maps show landmasses divided into regions such as countries and cities. Study a map of North America in an atlas or on the Internet. Then, draw a line to connect each city to its country. You will use each country more than once.

City	Country
1. Mexico City	
2. Toronto	Mexico
3. Washington, D.C.	
4. Montreal	
5. Chicago	Canada
6. Acapulco	
7. Boston	
8. Guadalajara	United States of America
9. Phoenix	
10. Vancouver	

Choose one country from the list above, or pick a country you are interested in studying. Do some research about this country. Then, write three facts about the country on the lines.

_____
_____
_____
_____

152 © Carson Dellosa Education

Social Studies Activity

Democratic Governments

Read the passage. Then, answer the questions.

There are many types of government. One type of government is a democratic government. A democratic government gives its citizens the power to make decisions.

The United States has a democratic government. In the United States, citizens elect a president. The president is the head of the government. The citizens also elect people to Congress. Congress is the branch of government that makes laws. Great Britain also has a democratic government. The prime minister is the head of the government in Great Britain. The prime minister also helps make laws.

1. There are many types of _____ .

2. A _____ government gives its citizens the power to make decisions.

3. In the United States, the _____ elect a president.

4. In the United States, the _____ is the head of the government.

5. Citizens of the United States also elect people to _____ .

6. Congress is the branch of government that makes _____ .

7. In Great Britain, the _____ helps make the laws.

8. What other kinds of government are there? Go to the library or go online with an adult to learn about a country that does not have a democratic government. How is that country's government similar to and different from yours?

_____

_____

_____

© Carson Dellosa Education

153

BONUS

Reflect and Reset

Think back on your year of second grade. What was the hardest part?

_____
_____
_____

What was your favorite part of second grade?

_____
_____
_____

What will you miss about second grade?

_____
_____
_____

What did you do in second grade that you are proud of?

_____
_____
_____

© Carson Dellosa Education

Reflect and Reset

BONUS

Look ahead to this coming year in third grade. What might be a challenge for you?

_____

_____

_____

What are you looking forward to in third grade?

_____

_____

_____

Set three goals for yourself for third grade. Maybe you want to join a new club or learn a new math skill. List your goals.

1. _____

2. _____

3. _____

Answer Key

Section 1
Day 1/Page 13

1. 45; **2.** 58; **3.** 881; **4.** 30; **5.** 362; **6.** 912; From left to right and top to bottom: zero, twenty, thirty, forty, sixty, eighty; **7.** Students should draw a triangle.; **8.** Students should draw a hexagon.; **9.** Students should draw a circle or an oval.; **10.** 700, 800, 900, 1,000, Rule: Add 100.; **11.** 50, 60, 70, 80, 90, 100, Rule: Add 10.; **12.** 25, 30, 35, 40, 45, 50, Rule: Add 5.; **13.** My grandma raises bees, but she has only been stung once.; **14.** Mr. Greene coaches our soccer team, and I think he does a great job.; **15.** The fireworks lit up the night sky, so everyone cheered.; **16.** Tanesha is moving to Illinois, but her family hasn't found a house yet.

Day 2/Page 15

1. 63¢; **2.** 52¢; **3.** 62¢; **4.** 51¢; **5.** 6, 6; **6.** 3, 3; **7.** 8, 8; **8.** 7, 7; **9.** pencil, sundae, helmet; **10.** rabbit, spider, tiger; **11.** puppy, candy, seven; **12.** wonder, cricket, marry; **13.** candle, muffin, circus; **14.** dollar, mitten, window; **15.** -oy words: toy, joy, loyal, enjoy, royal; -oi words: join, foil, boil, oink, oil

Day 3/Page 17

1. 346; **2.** 527; **3.** 831; **4.** 214; **5.** 428; **6.** 400; **7.** 680; **8.** 722; **9.** 399; **10.** Students should color 1 of 4 parts.; **11.** Students should color 2 of 3 parts.; **12.** Students should color 4 of 4 parts.; **13.** Students should color 1 of 3 parts.; **14.** Students should color 1 of 2 parts.; **15.** Students should color 3 of 4 parts.; **16.** C; **17.** to explain how insects and arachnids can be helpful; **18.** They move pollen from flower to flower.; **19.** They eat insects that chew on plants.; **20.** Crops are plants that farmers grow. The phrase "fruits and vegetables" is a clue.

Day 4/Page 19

1. <; **2.** >; **3.** >; **4.** <; **5.** <; **6.** >; **7.** >; **8.** <; **9.** <; **10.** 14, even; **11.** 9, odd; **12.** 18, even; **13.** 86; **14.** 62; **15.** 207; **16.** 124; **17.** 214; **18.** 195; **19.** 84; **20.** 168; **21.** S; **22.** L; **23.** S; **24.** L; **25.** S; **26.** S; **27.** L; **28.** S; **29.** L; **30.** L; **31.** S; **32.** L

Day 5/Page 21

1. 9 ones; **2.** 2 hundreds; **3.** 1 ten; **4.** 3 tens; **5.** 3 hundreds; **6.** 0 tens; **7.** Students should divide the circle into 4 equal parts, fourth.; **8.** Students should divide the triangle into 2 equal parts, half.; **9.** Students should divide the rectangle into 3 equal parts, third.; **10.** 25; **11.** 122; **12.** 60; **13.** 435; **14.** 142; **15.** 99; **16.** short; **17.** long; **18.** short; **19.** long; **20.** long; **21.** short; **22.** long; **23.** short; **24.** short; **25.** long

Day 6/Page 23

1. 629, 637, 682; **2.** 879, 429, 609, 509; **3.** 231, 38, 639, 530; **4.** 354, 151, 555, 250, 658; **5.** 423, 484, 432; **6.** 327, 147, 607, 447; **7.** Austin, Texas; **8.** Hanukkah; **9.** Iceland; **10.** Papa Pete's; **11.** Nashville, Tennessee; **12.** Crunch Os; **13.** Kwanzaa; **14.** A; **15.** travel quickly and easily from one coast of the United States to the other; **16.** eastern and western parts of the country; **17.** a golden nail; **18.** Answers will vary, but may include that railroads helped carry people and goods and connected the two coasts of the United States.

Day 7/Page 25

Book measurements will vary, but each should be rounded to the nearest whole inch and recorded on the line plot.; **Holidays:** Memorial Day, Veterans Day, Juneteenth; **Products:** Squeaky Clean soap, Clarabelle's pies, Sweet Orchard fruit; **Places:** Ukraine, Rocky Mountains, Mexico City, St. Louis; **1.** 500 + 20 + 8; **2.** 100 + 30 + 0 (ones); **3.** 600 + 80 + 9; **4.** 400 + 20 + 1; **5.** 700 + 0 (tens) + 8; **6.** 500 + 60 + 7; **7.** 900 + 60 + 3; **8.** 800 + 0 (tens) + 6; Students' writing will vary.

Day 8/Page 27

1. 3 inches, 7 centimeters; **2.** 4 inches, 9 centimeters; **3.** 2 inches, 6 centimeters; **4.** Students should circle loudly and underline barked.; **5.** Students should circle everywhere and underline looked.; **6.** Students should circle faster and underline swims.; **7.** Students should circle slowly and underline walked.; **8.** Students should circle early and underline awoke.; **9.** Students should circle outside and underline play.; **10.** re-, D; **11.** un-, B; **12.** mis-, A; **13.** un-, E; **14.** mis-, C; **15.** 2, 2; **16.** 4, 2; **17.** 1, 1; **18.** 3, 3; **19.** 2, 1; **20.** 1, 1; **21.** 2, 2; **22.** 2, 2; **23.** 3, 3; **24.** 2, 2

Day 9/Page 29

1. 6 + 5 = 11, 5 + 6 = 11, 11 – 6 = 5, 11 – 5 = 6; **2.** 4 + 5 = 9, 5 + 4 = 9, 9 – 5 = 4, 9 – 4 = 5; **3.** 7 + 5 = 12, 5 + 7 = 12, 12 – 7 = 5, 12 – 5 = 7; **4.** Students should divide the rectangle into 3 rows and 5 columns, 15.; **5.** Students should divide the rectangle into 4 rows and 6 columns, 24.; **6.** Students should divide the rectangle into 2 rows and 7 columns, 14.; **7.** -less; **8.** -ness; **9.** -less; **10.** -ness; **11.** -ness; **12.** -ness; Words in the fly column: dry, eye, sky; Words in the baby column: city, happy, story

Day 10/Page 31

1. +; **2.** –; **3.** –; **4.** =; **5.** +; **6.** –; **7.** –; **8.** –; **9.** =; **10.** –; **11.** =; **12.** +; **13.** +; **14.** +; **15.** –; **16.** 5 + 5 + 5 + 5 = 20; **17.** 3 + 3 + 3 + 3 = 15; **18.** 8 + 8 = 16; **19.** 7 + 7 + 7 = 21; **20.** house/boat; **21.** rain/drop; **22.** light/house; **23.** door/bell; **24.** barn/yard; **25.** bed/room; **26.** snow/flakes; **27.** enlarge; **28.** prefer; **29.** proud

Day 11/Page 33

1. 63 marbles; **2.** 24 apples; **3.** 63 minutes; **4.** 67 puppies; **5.** gulped; **6.** shattered; **7.** gobble; **8.** furious; **9.** tapped; **10.** B, A; **11.** A, B; **12.** B, A; **13.** B, A; Students should circle the following words: zoo, hoop, soon, pool, scoop, cool, stool, food, moon, moose, goose.; Students should draw Xs on the following words: book, wool, cook, hood, took, brook, foot, wood, crook.

Day 12/Page 35

1. C; **2.** A; **3.** H; **4.** B; **5.** D; **6.** E; **7.** I; **8.** J; **9.** F; **10.** G; **11.** men; **12.** teeth; **13.** leaves; **14.** geese; **15.** knives; **16.** mice; **17.** Students should write the following words under animals: fox, elephant, bear, deer.; Students should write the following words under tools: saw, pliers, hammer, screwdriver.; Students should write the following words under clothing: shirt, pants, socks, hat.; **18.** colony; **19.** fleet; **20.** swarm; **21.** bouquet; **22.** school

Day 13/Page 37

1. 40 students; **2.** 20 more students; **3.** Cats and No Pets; **4.** 60 students; **5.** Taylor's; **6.** computer's; **7.** grandma's; **8.** Ana's; **9.** C; **10.** as long as it takes to sing the alphabet; **11.** washes away germs that make you sick; **12.** B

Day 14/Page 39

1. 758; **2.** 599; **3.** 851; **4.** 320; **5.** 516; **6.** 466; **7.** 904; **8.** 171; **9.** 1,000; **10.** 1; **11.** 95, Students should mark the number line beginning on 60 and ending on 95.; **12.** 36, Students should mark the number line beginning on 22 and ending on 36.; **13.** 70, Students should mark the number line beginning on 100 and ending on 70.; **14.** I planted seeds.; **15.** Luke started his car.; **16.** I put on my socks.; **17.** We built a snowman.; **18.** I put toothpaste on my toothbrush.; **19.** I climbed into bed.; Students' writing will vary.

Day 15/Page 41

1. <, =, >; **2.** =, <, >; **3.** <, =, =; **4.** =, <, <; **5.** =, <, =; **6.** >, <, =; **7.** dis<u>obey</u> = not obey; **8.** re<u>appear</u> = appear again; **9.** un<u>lucky</u> = not lucky; **10.** dis<u>honest</u> = not honest; **11.** pre<u>order</u> = order before; **12.** un<u>safe</u> = not safe; **13.** C; **14.** C

156

Answer Key

Day 16/Page 43
1. 34 flowers; **2.** 84 laps; **3.** 32 cars; **4.** 43 toys; **5.** 34 centimeters; **6.** 6 inches; **7.** 153 meters; **8.** 39 pounds; **9.** A; **10.** Drops of water rise into the air.; **11.** when the air cools; **12.** They produce rain, snow, sleet, or hail.; **13.** The author's purpose is to provide information about the water cycle.

Day 17/Page 45
1. 42; **2.** 24; **3.** 89; **4.** 14; **5.** 78; **6.** 12; **7.** 13; **8.** 0; **9.** 35; **10.** 48; **11.** 86; **12.** 97; **13.** 6; **14.** 14; **15.** 11; **16.** myself; **17.** themselves; **18.** himself; **19.** itself; **20.** herself; **21.** B; **22.** A; **23.** phone; **24.** elephants; **25.** alphabet; **26.** amphibian

Day 18/Page 47
1. 449; **2.** 997; **3.** 589; **4.** 338; **5.** 472; **6.** 757; **7.** 813; **8.** 747; **9.** 804; **10.** 288; **11.** 871; **12.** 895; **13.** 407; **14.** 800; **15.** 682; **16.** unsure, not sure; **17.** unhappy, not happy; **18.** unable, not able; **19.** rewrite, write again; Students' writing will vary.;

20. ; **21.** ; **22.** ; **23.** , 5:50; **24.** , 12:10

Day 19/Page 49
1. 598; **2.** 100; **3.** 582; **4.** 813; **5.** 107; **6.** 478; **7.** 422; **8.** 760; **9.** 72; **10.** 56; **11.** C; **12.** B; **13.** jump into bed too; **14.** the boy; **15.** everywhere the boy goes; **16.** Yes, it has a steady beat because the syllables of the words form a pattern.; **17.** w; **18.** b; **19.** k; **20.** k; **21.** k, gh; **22.** b

Day 20/Page 51
1. 389; **2.** 855; **3.** 363; **4.** 388; **5.** 106; **6.** 59; **7.** 301; **8.** 203; **9.** 605; **10.** 778; **11.** 993; **12.** 790; **13.** 999; **14.** 900; **15.** 840; Students should write the following words under present: blow, find, fly, know, laugh, wear, write.; Students should write the following words under past: blew, found, flew, knew, laughed, wore, wrote.; **16.** F; **17.** R; **18.** R; **19.** F; **20.** F; **21.** R; **22.** F; **23.** R; **24.** F; **25.** F; Students' writing will vary.

Bonus Page 54
the marble that traveled through water; Answers will vary.

Bonus Page 55
Yellow Sands

Bonus Page 56

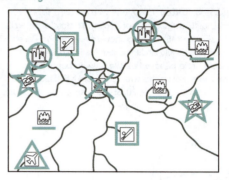

Bonus Page 57
1. Shady Oaks Street; **2.** Clear Creek Road; **3.** Main Street; **4.** Windy Way; **5.** Walnut Street; **6.** Shady Oaks Street and Park Street

Section 2
Day 1/Page 61
1. 111; **2.** 115; **3.** 47; **4.** 114; **5.** 111; **6.** 82; **7.** 120; **8.** 112; **9.** 132; **10.** 83; **11.** 50; **12.** 41; **13.** 124; **14.** 58; **15.** 95; **16.** slept; **17.** held; **18.** made; **19.** won; **20.** left; **21.** fell; **22.** bought; **23.** Dion's baseball mitt; **24.** Jasper's soccer ball; **25.** Trinity's goggles; **26.** Grandpa's golf clubs; **27.** Cassidy's ballet shoes; **28.** correct; **29.** incorrect; **30.** incorrect; **31.** correct; **32.** incorrect

Day 2/Page 63
1. 13; **2.** 49; **3.** 45; **4.** 8; **5.** 56; **6.** 59; **7.** 17; **8.** 39; **9.** 75; **10.** 15; **11.** 46; **12.** 19; **13.** made; **14.** took; **15.** bought; **16.** saw; **17.** went; **18.** flew; **19.** A; **20.** C; **21.** play outside, go swimming

Day 3/Page 65
1. 451; **2.** 734; **3.** 839; **4.** 448; **5.** 682; **6.** 526; **7.** 225; **8.** 381; **9.** 628; **10.** 992; **11.** am; **12.** is; **13.** are; **14.** am; **15.** are; **16.** is; **17.** are; **18.** 3 × 4 = 12; **19.** 6 × 3 = 18; **20.** 3 × 10 = 30; **21.** 7 × 4 = 28; **22.** 10; **23.** 6; **24.** 7; **25.** 16; **26.** 8; **27.** 4; **28.** 25; **29.** 9; **30.** 4

Day 4/Page 67
1. 5 × 3 = 15; **2.** 7 × 4 = 28; **3.** 5 × 1 = 5; **4.** 2 × 3 = 6; **5.** noun; **6.** adverb; **7.** adjective; **8.** verb; **9.** pronoun; **10.** verb; **11.** Students should mark $\frac{3}{4}$ on the number line.; **12.** Students should mark $\frac{5}{8}$ on the number line.; **13.** Students should mark $\frac{1}{3}$ on the number line.; **14.** Students should mark 1 on the number line.

81 Riverwood Rd.
Charlotte , NC 28870

1425 Newtown Terrace #12
Providence , RI 02906

132 West Billingsley Lane
Taos , NM 87571

21896 Langston Blvd.
San Diego , CA 92119

Day 5/Page 69
1. ✓; **2.** X; **3.** ✓; **4.** X; **5.** ✓; **6.** X; **7.** X; **8.** ✓; **9.** X; **10.** ✓; **11.** ✓; **12.** ✓; **13.** have; **14.** has; **15.** have; **16.** has; **17.** B; **18.** F; **19.** T; **20.** T; **21.** F; **22.** Students' paragraphs will vary.

Answer Key

Day 6/Page 71

1. 1:25; **2.** 11:07; **3.** 3:56; **4.** 2:38; **5.** 10:40; **6.** 7:22; **7.** one who gardens; **8.** not honest; **9.** process of adding; **10.** not stick; **11.** not healthy; **12.** state of being ill; **13.** one who collects; **14.** use again; **15.** Students should circle *reason*. Possible answer: *reasoning*; **16.** Students should circle *interest*. Possible answer: *interests*; **17.** Students should circle *behave*. Possible answer: *behaved*; **18.** Students should circle *believ*. Possible answer: *believable*; **19.** Students should circle *cycl*. Possible answer: *unicycle*; **20.** Students should circle *phone*. Possible answer: *phonograph*; Students' writing will vary.

Day 7/Page 73:

7. raked, raking; **8.** jumped, jumping; **9.** hugged, hugging; **10.** cooked, cooking; **11.** skated, skating; **12.** wrapped, wrapping; **13.** sneezed, sneezing; **14.** popped, popping; **15.** talked, talking; **16.** smiled, smiling; **17.** C; **18.** E; **19.** D; **20.** B; **21.** A; **22.** 24 in.; **23.** 15 in.; **24.** 20 cm; **25.** 43 in.

Day 8/Page 75

1. 7:50; **2.** 4:45; **3.** 6:50; **4.** 11:30; **5.** went; **6.** gone; **7.** went; **8.** gone; **9.** more than 900; **10.** insects, fruit, and nectar; **11.** 16 inches (40 cm) in length; **12.** The main idea of the first paragraph is that bats help people in many ways.; **13.** The author provides the following evidence to support the main idea: bats eat insects, and bats pollinate and spread the seeds of many plants. **14.** mosquitoes, mayflies, and moths

Day 9/Page 77

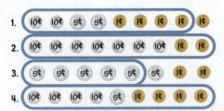

5. stop, stopping, stopped; **6.** clap, clapping, clapped; **7.** hopping, hopped, hop; **8.** 60; **9.** 140; **10.** 30; **11.** 290; **12.** 10; **13.** 300; **14.** 600; **15.** 200; **16.** 700; **17.** 800; **18.** odd **19.** even; **20.** even; **21.** odd; **22.** even; **23.** odd; **24.** even; **25.** odd; **26.** odd

Day 10/Page 79

Students should draw 4 loaves for January, 4 loaves for February, 6 loaves for March, 8 loaves for April, $8\frac{1}{2}$ loaves for May, and $9\frac{1}{2}$ loaves for June.; Yesterday, we **learned** about colors in art. We **made** a color wheel. We found out that there **are** three basic colors. They **are** called *primary colors*. Red, yellow, and blue are primary colors. Primary colors mix to make other colors. Red and yellow **make** orange. Yellow and blue make green. Blue and red make purple. Orange, green, and purple **are** secondary colors.; **1.** B; **2.** A; **3.** B; **4.** A; **5.** A; **6.** 180; **7.** 350; **8.** 360; **9.** 240; **10.** 240; **11.** 270; **12.** 480; **13.** 80; **14.** 60; **15.** 70

Day 11/Page 81:

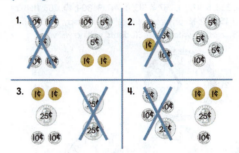

5. equal; **6.** tiny; **7.** low; **8.** rainy; **9.** B; **10.** Africa, Antarctica, Asia, Australia, Europe, North America, South America; **11.** millions of years ago; **12.** They were once one piece of land.

Day 12/Page 83

1.–6. Answers will vary.; **7.** big, red; **8.** soft; **9.** steep; **10.** screechy; **11.** 260, 300, 200 + 50 + 6; **12.** 540, 500, 500 + 40 + 2; **13.** 310, 300, 300 + 10 + 1; **14.** 900, 900, 800 + 90 + 8; **15.** 430, 400, 400 + 20 + 6; **16.** 660, 700, 600 + 50 + 7; **17.** 100, 100, 100 + 2; Students' writing will vary.

Day 13/Page 85

1. 3 × $3 = $9, $20 − $9 = $11; **2.** 6 × 2 = 12, 12 + 4 = 16 packets; **3.** 8 × 6 = 48, 55 − 48 = 7 grapes; **4.** 27 ÷ 9 = 3, 12 × 3 = 36 yards; **5.** blue, yellow; **6.** little, green; **7.** colorful, soft; **8.** dark, gray; **9.** new, brown; **10.** 2, 1, 4, 3; **11.** opinion; **12.** fact; **13.** opinion; **14.** fact

Day 14/Page 87

1. 1 + 3 + 1 = 5 inches; **2.** 3 + 2 + 1 = 6 inches; **3.** 1 + 4 + 2 = 7 inches; Students' writing will vary.; **4.** A; **5.** 8–11 hours each night; **6.** You might have trouble paying attention to your teacher.; **7.** read a book; **8.** C

Day 15/Page 89

1. 7 cm; **2.** 8 cm; **3.** 9 cm; **4.** 3 cm; **5.** 5 cm; **6.–10.** Answers will vary.; **11.** C; **12.** B; Students' writing will vary.

Day 16/Page 91

1. B; **2.** A; **3.** B; **4.** A; **5.** B; **6.** B; **7.** hasn't; **8.** I'm; **9.** you'll; **10.** wouldn't; **11.** we've; **12.** we'd; **13.** you're; **14.** she's; **15.** isn't; **16.** I'll; **17.** page 4; **18.** Chapter 3; **19.** page 26; **20.** All About Ants; **21.** electric; **22.** train; **23.** keep; **24.** truck; **25.** play

Day 17/Page 93

1. C; **2.** B; **3.** B; **4.** A; **5.** she is; **6.** they are; **7.** are not; **8.** you have; **9.** I have; **10.** I would; **11.** it is; **12.** have not; **13.** she will; **14.** should not; **15.** C; **16.** B; **17.** A; **18.** B

Day 18/Page 95

1. 5; **2.** 7; **3.** 3; **4.** They've; **5.** We'll; **6.** I'll; **7.** We've; **8.** We're; **9.** B; **10.** M; **11.** B; **12.** J; **13.** M; **14.** J; **15.** B; **16.** B; **17.** J; **18.** B; **19.** E; **20.** A; **21.** D; **22.** F; **23.** C; **24.** B

Answer Key

Day 19/Page 97

1. Year, Billy, Miller; 2. Matilda; 3. Schoolhouse Rock; 4. Worry, Be, Happy; 5. Wild; 6. Walking, After, Midnight; 7. December—Dec., Doctor—Dr., Thursday—Thurs., ounce—oz.; 8. October—Oct., foot— ft., Avenue—Ave., Road—Rd.; 9. yard—yd., March—Mar., inch—in., Wednesday—Wed.; 10. Senior—Sr., Monday—Mon., Fahrenheit—F, Street—St.; 11. pride; 12. childhood; 13. kindness; 14. delight; 15. honesty; 16. truth; Students' writing will vary.

Day 20/Page 99

1. Students should draw a square.; 2. Students should draw a rectangle.; 3. Students should draw a rhombus (diamond).; 4. Students should draw any shape with four sides that does not fit the definition of a square, rectangle, or rhombus.; 5. A; 6. C; 7. B; 8. C; 9. A; 10. It means that both trees and grass are good things for humans that come from nature.;

11.

Alike or Different?	Grass	Tree
living thing	X	X
stands straight in the wind		X
bends in the wind	X	
tall		X
small	X	
can be climbed		X
can be sat on	X	
green in color	X	X

Bonus Page 103

1. B,2; 2. H,1; 3. G,5; 4. B,6; 5. E,1; 6. D,4; 7. A,4; 8. E,5

Bonus Page 104

Bonus Page 105

1. C, Africa; 2. A, North America; 3. D, Europe; 4. B, South America; 5. E, Asia; 6. G, Antarctica; 7. F, Australia

Section 3
Day 1/Page 109

1. Possible answers: The shapes are similar because they both have four sides and four corners. The shapes are different because the square's sides are all equal and the rectangle's sides are not equal.; 2. Possible answers: The shapes are similar because they are both two-dimensional. The shapes are different because the triangle has three sides and the square has four sides.; 3. Possible answers: The shapes are similar because they both have no sides. The shapes are different because the circle is round and the oval is not round.; 4. Possible answers: The shapes are similar because they both have four equal sides. The shapes are different because the square has straight corners and the rhombus does not.; 5. are; 6. spots; 7. sees; 8. drops; 9. gather; 10. B; 11. C; Answers may vary. Possible answers: 12. Although; 13. and; 14. Whether; 15. but

Day 2/Page 111

1. tries; 2. happiness; 3. sitting; 4. hopped; 5. smiled; 6. sliding; 7. lying; 8. puppies; 9. 35 square feet; 10. 160 square feet; 11. 72 square feet; 12. 15 square feet; Students' writing will vary.

Day 3/Page 113

1. 365; 2. 577; 3. 575; 4. 893; 5. 696; 6. 646; 7. 634; 8. 343; 9. 252; 10. 225; 11. 716; 12. 840; 13. 819; 14. 649; 15. 739; 16. F; 17. N; 18. P; 19. F; 20. N; 21. N; 22. P; 23. P; 24. A; 25. C; 26. A

Day 4/Page 115

1. Students should divide the square into 4 equal parts, $\frac{1}{4}$.; 2. Students should divide the rectangle into 6 equal parts, $\frac{1}{6}$.; 3. Students should divide the circle into 3 equal parts, $\frac{1}{3}$.; 4. Is the busy mail carrier leaving?; 5. Is that man Felix's neighbor?; 6. Can she ride her new bike?; 7. Will I ride the black horse?; 8. paw; 9. math; 10. bison; 11. hand; 12. race; 13. color these words blue: space, mice, dance, bounce, lace, fence, cent, cell, face; color these words orange: page, large, rage, cage, ginger, gentle, bridge, judge, age, germ, giraffe

Day 5/Page 117

1. 8 × 4 = 32 square units; 2. 6 × 2 = 12 square units; 3. 5 × 3 = 15 square units; 4. 10 × 5 = 50 square units; 5. I; 6. E; 7. E; 8. D; 9. Watch out!; 10. I had a great day!; From left to right: pink, purple, white, orange, yellow; 11. faster, fastest; 12. tall, taller; 13. cold, coldest; 14. brighter; 15. deep, deepest

Day 6/Page 119

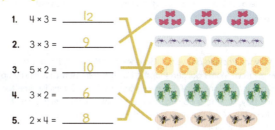

6. IM; 7. IM; 8. E; 9. IM; 10. IM; 11. D; 12. I; 13. E; 14. A; 15. left column: 3, 1; right column: 2, 4

Day 7/Page 121

1. 5; 2. 25; 3. 12; 4. 0; 5. 4; 6. 20; 7. 15; 8. 1; 9. 10; 10. 7; 11. 8; 12. 6; 13. 9; 14. 0; 15.–18. Answers will vary.; 19. noun; 20. a bud or a seed; 21. after; 22. Answers will vary.; 23. birds; 24. school supplies; 25. animals; 26. drinks

Day 8/Page 123

1. 3 × 4 = 12 flowers; 2. 4 × 5 = 20 pieces; 3. 3 × 2 = 6 straws; 4. 4 × 4 = 16 chairs; 5. them; 6. their; 7. them; 8. his; 9. it; 10. her; 11. She got up late today.; 12. She missed the bus.; 13. Answers will vary.; Students' writing will vary.

Day 9/Page 125

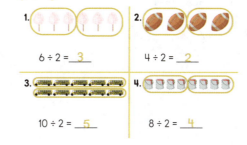

Answer Key

5. C; **6.** S; **7.** CX; **8.** S; **9.** CX; **10.** Laiana is very busy in the summer.; **11.** eight o'clock; **12.** She helps him work in the garden.; **13.** Answers will vary but may include: swimming, playing soccer, reading, playing with friends, and riding her bike.; **14.** more joyfully; **15.** latest; **16.** more softly; **17.** farthest; **18.** most brightly

Day 10/Page 127

1. >; **2.** <; **3.** >; **4.** >; **5.** >; **6.** <; **7.** An Exciting Camping Trip; **8.** My Ride on a Donkey; **9.** The Day I Missed School; **10.** Fun, Fabulous Pets; **11.** A Fire Drill; **12.** My Summer Job; **13.** 24; **14.** 18; **15.** 18; **16.** 30; **17.** overjoyed, happy; **18.** cross, furious; **19.** large, gigantic

Day 11/Page 129

1. 6; **2.** 6; **3.** 7; **4.** 9; **5.** 7; **6.** 7; **7.** 9; **8.** 9; Mom, Dad, and I went camping last week. We went with Uncle Louis and Aunt Greta. We had fun. Dad and Uncle Louis climbed on rocks. Aunt Greta and I saw a chipmunk. We all hiked on exciting trails. There was only one problem. Mom, Dad, and I did not bring sweaters. Dad said that it would be warm in the desert. He was wrong. At night, it was very cold. Uncle Louis and Aunt Greta had sweaters. Mom, Dad, and I stayed close to the fire. Next time, we will bring warmer clothes.; **9.** Dad thought that the author would be warm in the desert.; **10.** The story is told from a child's point of view.; **11.** They stay close to the fire.; **12.** reality; **13.** fantasy; **14.** reality; **15.** fantasy; **16.** 7; **17.** 18; **18.** 28; **19.** 9; **20.** 5; **21.** 7; **22.** 7; **23.** 5

Day 12/Page 131

1. $\frac{5}{1}$; **2.** $\frac{11}{1}$; **3.** $\frac{24}{1}$; **4.** $\frac{9}{1}$; **5.** 4; **6.** 8; **7.** 12; **8.** 5; **9.** "Did you know that Reid lives in Dallas, Texas?"; **10.** "Mr. Jarvis is my neighbor," said Grandma.; **11.** "Is Nasir's birthday in April?" asked Sasha.; **12.** "My mother and I shop at Smith's Market," I added.; **13.** B; **14.** The author gives the information in time order.; **15.** It was bright yellow.; **16.** She was the first woman to fly alone across the Atlantic Ocean.; **17.** She decided to fly around the world. Her plane was lost over the Pacific Ocean.

Day 13/Page 133

Answers will vary. Possible answers: **1.** Go ahead and tell me, I'm all ears.; **2.** You can tell from Mom's garden that she has a green thumb.; **3.** Hurry up! It's time to get the ball rolling.; **4.** I know it's only 8:00, but I think it's time for me to hit the hay.; **5.** Where do birds live?; **6.** My sister works very hard.; **7.** She can swim like a fish./ Can she swim like a fish?; **8.** Why is grass green?; **9.** B; **10.** C; **11.** E; **12.** F; **13.** A; **14.** D; **15.** B; **16.** G; **17.** H

Day 14/Page 135

1. Students should mark $\frac{1}{2}$ and $\frac{3}{6}$ on the number lines.; **2.** Students should mark $\frac{2}{3}$ and $\frac{4}{6}$ on the number lines.; **3.** Each pair of fractions shown is equivalent.; Possible answers: **4.** Mr. Sanchez is a teacher, but he doesn't work at my school.; **5.** Mom is teaching Omar how to mow the lawn, but Nabil is too young.; **6.** Hannah feeds the cats each morning, or they meow until she wakes up.; **7.** It is supposed to snow on Tuesday, so I'm hoping school is canceled.; **8.** Beatrix just joined the swim team, and her first swim meet is in July.; **9.** 26; **10.** 31; **11.** 15; **12.** 21; **13.** 60; **14.** 42; Students' writing will vary.

Day 15/Page 137

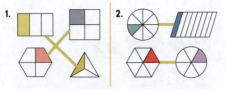

3. is very busy; **4.** quit, be done; **5.** study, read; **6.** told the news/secret; **7.** likes to stay up late; **8.** C; **9.** all citizens over the age of 18; **10.** 1920; **11.** Adults of all races were given the right to vote.; **12.** People can help decide who serves in the government and what kinds of laws are passed.

Day 16/Page 139

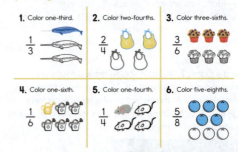

The Earth has many mountains, rivers, lakes, oceans, and continents. The Andes, the Rockies, and the Urals are mountain ranges. The Amazon, the Nile, and the Hudson are rivers. Lake Erie, Lake Ontario, and Lake Huron are three of the Great Lakes. The Pacific, the Atlantic, and the Arctic are oceans. Europe, Asia, and Africa are continents. New Zealand, Greenland, and Iceland are islands.; **7.** Travis; **8.** Keisha; **9.** Lamar; **10.** Mrs. Travers; **11.** Friday; **12.** 5; **13.** 26; **14.** Friday

Day 17/Page 141

Students' writing will vary.; **1.** Bobby has a dog named Shadow.; **2.** Do bluebirds eat insects?; **3.** Can I borrow your video game?; **4.** My name is Nikki.; **5.** water; **6.** ground; **7.** trees; **8.** window; **9.** cow; **10.** cat; **11.** slowly; **12.** red; **13.** heavy; **14.** tightly

Day 18/Page 143

1. hot dogs and fries; **2.** fruit bowls; **3.** 20; **4.** 10; **5.–7.** Answers will vary.; **8.** $\frac{1}{2}$ and $\frac{2}{4}$; **9.** $\frac{4}{6}$ and $\frac{2}{3}$; **10.** $\frac{4}{4}$ and $\frac{1}{1}$; **11.** $\frac{1}{3}$ and $\frac{3}{9}$; Students' writing will vary.

Day 19/Page 145

1. April, June, July; **2.** 4.5 inches; **3.** February; Students' writing will vary.; **4.** 5; **5.** 1; **6.** 4; **7.** 2; **8.** 3; Students' writing will vary.

Day 20/Page 147

1. 2; **2.** 16; **3.** Beth; **4.** Sue and Lori; **5.** Dante; vegetables, noun; They, pronoun; crunchy, adjective; love, verb; boils, verb; yellow, adjective; **6.** B; **7.** win the play-off game; **8.** A

Bonus Page 149

It looks like they mix together.; They separate.

Bonus Page 151

1. A; **2.** C; **3.** F; **4.** H; **5.** E; **6.** G; **7.** B; **8.** I; **9.** D

Bonus Page 152

1. Mexico; **2.** Canada; **3.** United States of America; **4.** Canada; **5.** United States of America; **6.** Mexico; **7.** United States of America; **8.** Mexico; **9.** United States of America; **10.** Canada; Facts will vary.

Bonus Page 153

1. government; **2.** democratic; **3.** citizens; **4.** president; **5.** Congress; **6.** laws; **7.** prime minister; **8.** Students' writing will vary.

noun	pronoun	verb
adjective	adverb	collective noun
reflexive pronoun	irregular plural noun	contraction

describes an action or state of being **jump** **talk** **eat**	takes the place of a noun **I** **he/she** **they, them** **it**	names a person, place, or thing **teacher** **park** **dog**
a group of people, animals, or things **class** **litter** **bunch**	describes a verb, adjective, or adverb **quickly** **well** **soon**	describes a noun or pronoun **blue** **good** **heavy**
a shortened form of two words put together **I'm** **they're** **it's**	a plural noun that doesn't follow the *add -s or -es* rule **teeth** **mice** **wolves**	a pronoun that ends in *-self* or *-selves*, refers back to the subject **myself** **themselves** **itself**

© Carson Dellosa

pre-	dis-	re-
past form of **run**	past form of **think**	past form of **do**
past form of **see**	past form of **eat**	past form of **cut**

again	not	before
redo replace replay	disagree dislike disbelief	premade preschool presale
did	thought	ran
cut	ate	saw

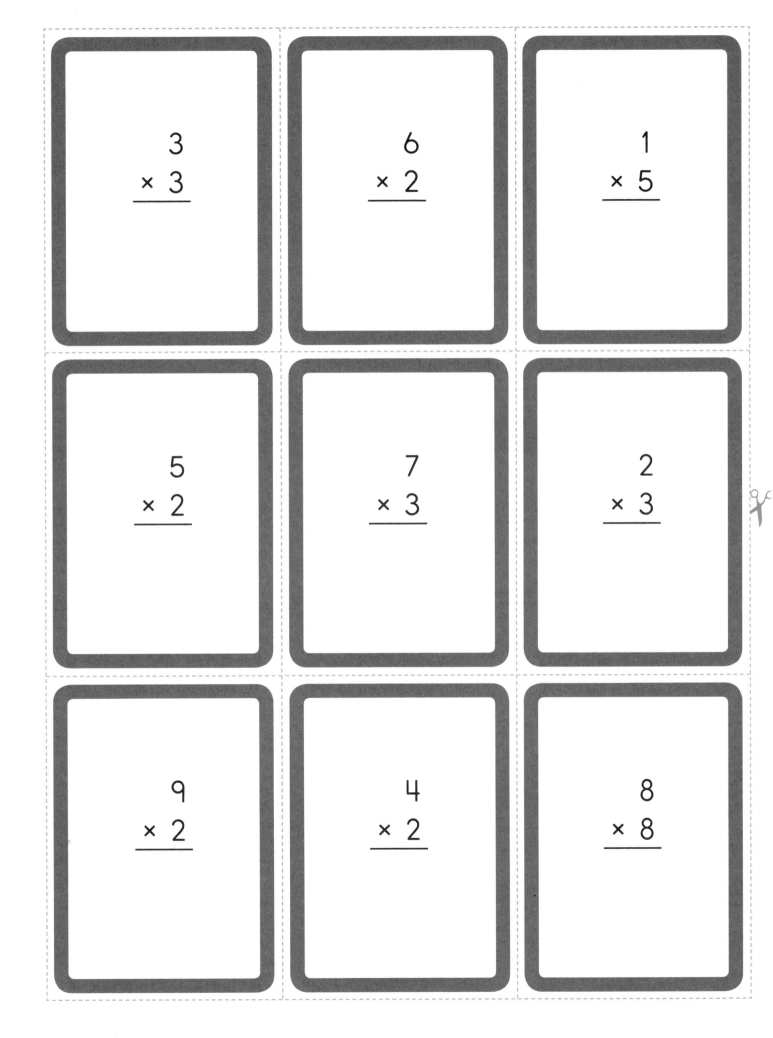

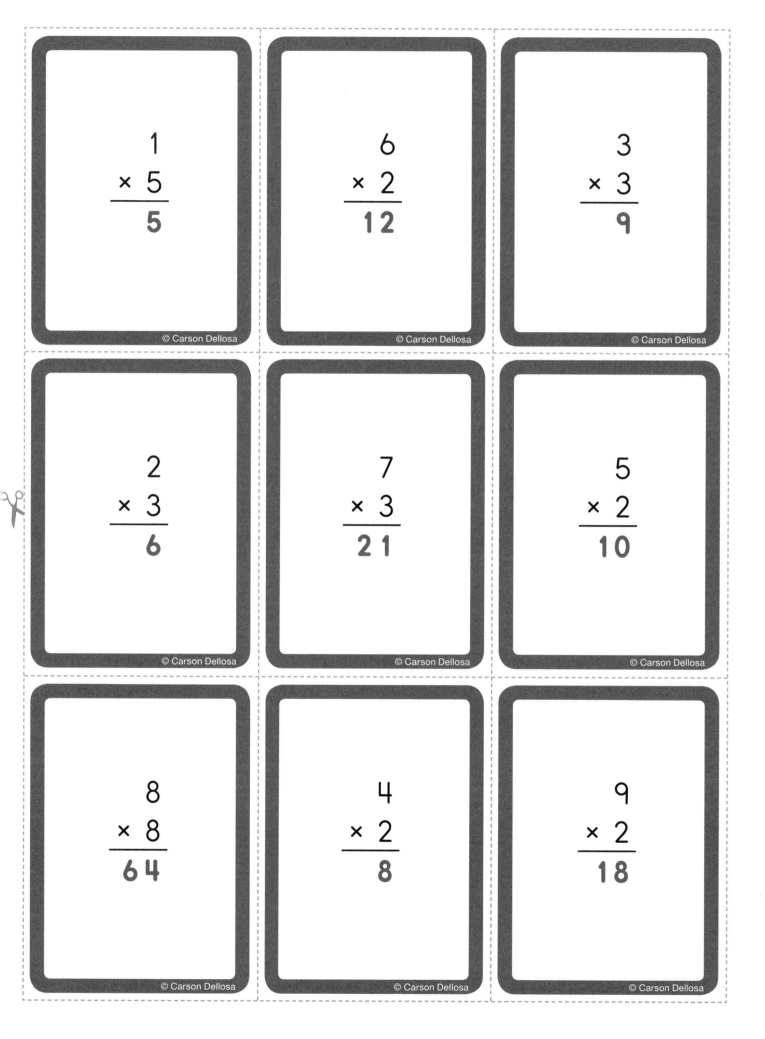

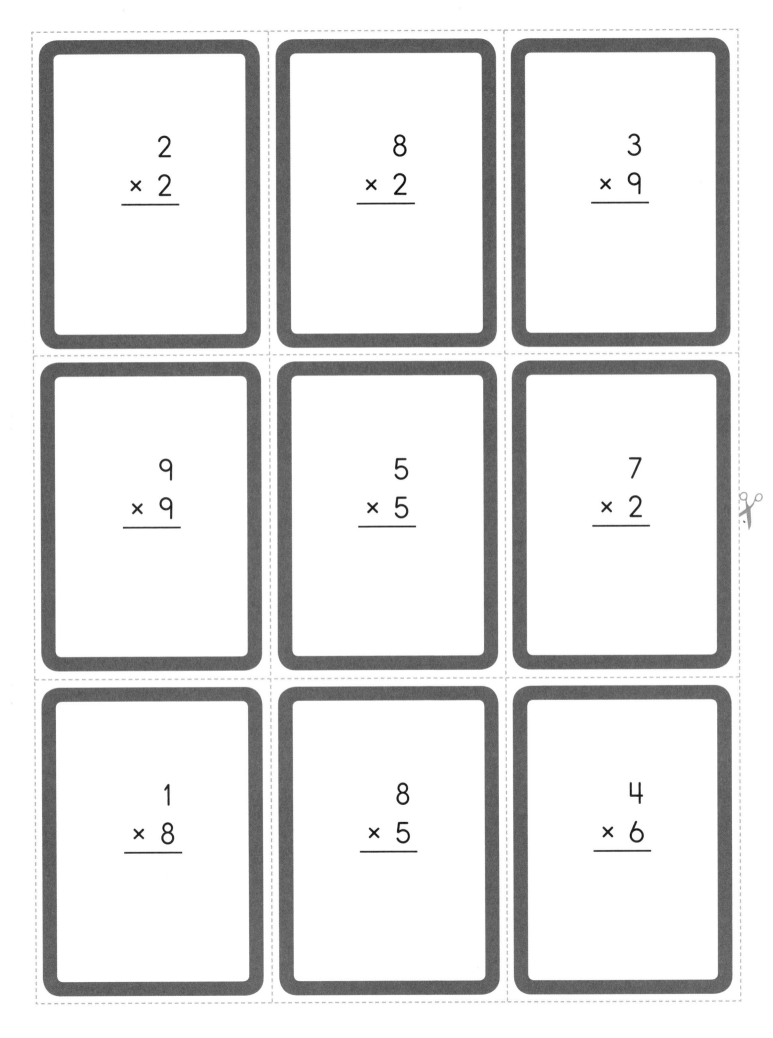

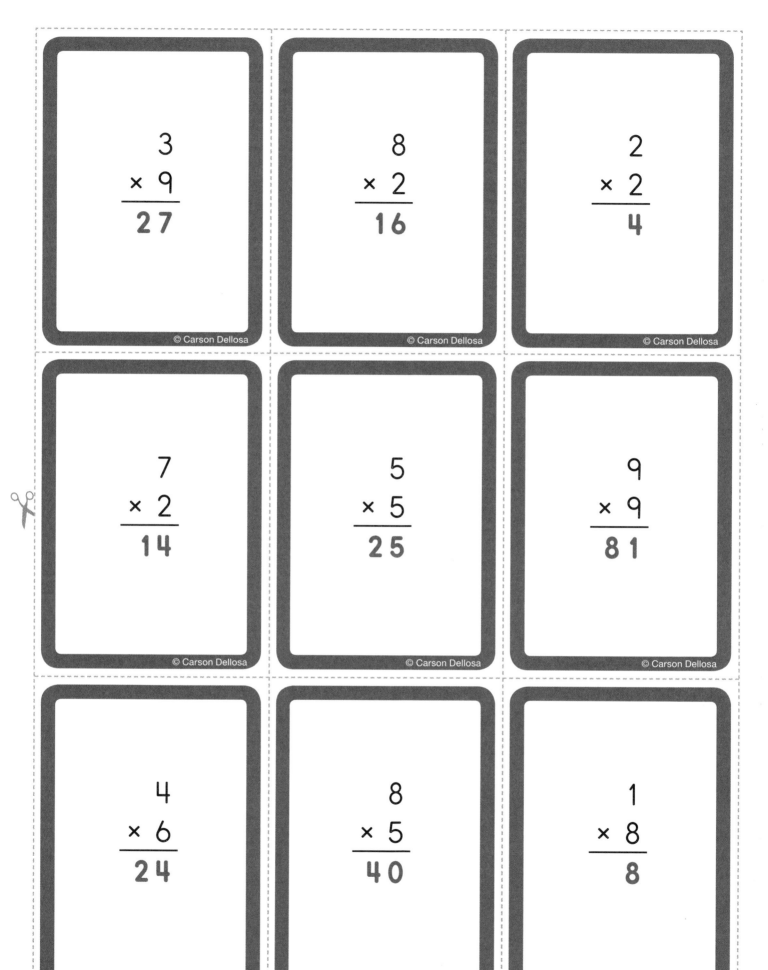

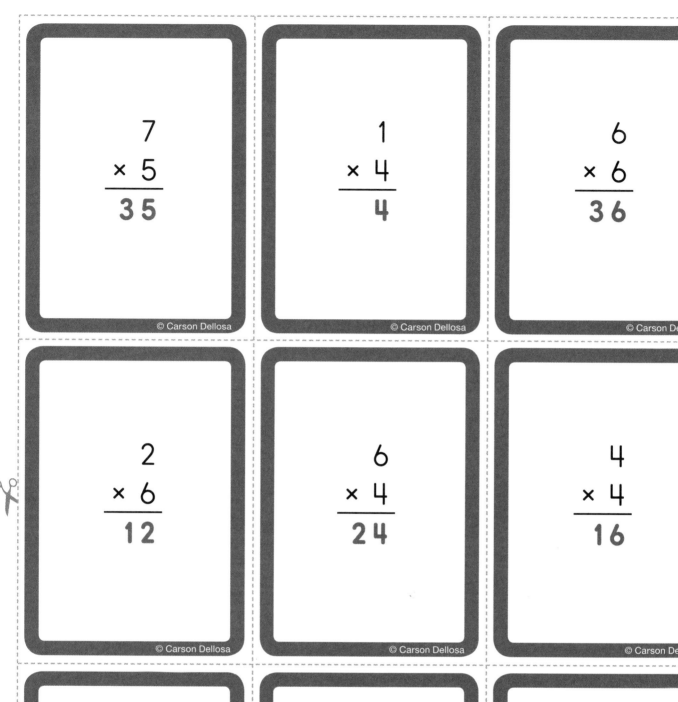

30¢	10¢	5¢
$1.50	$1.00	50¢
50¢	30¢	$1.40

Cut out the fraction pieces. Use the pieces to find equivalent fractions.

© Carson Dellosa

This page has been intentionally left blank.

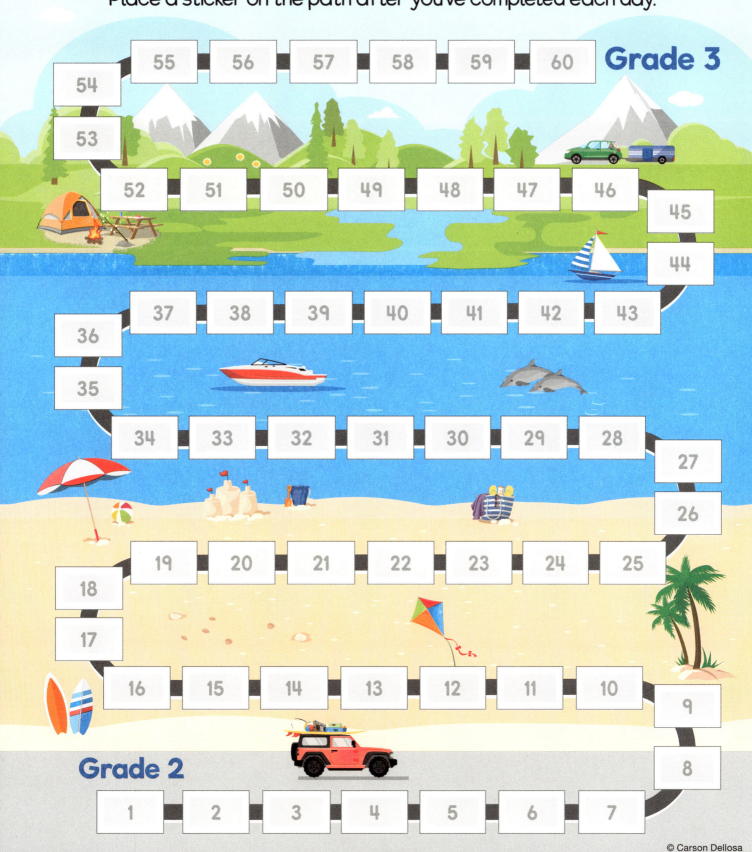

Place Value

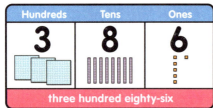

How to Tell Time

STEP 1
Find the Hour

Look at the short hand. What number has it passed?

STEP 2
Find the Minutes

Look at the long hand. Start at the 12 and count by 5s. Then, count on by 1s.

Length

An **inch** is about . . .
- knuckle
- paper clip
- 25¢ quarter

A **foot** is about . . .
- ruler
- fingertip to elbow

A **centimeter** is about . . .
- eraser
- fingertip

A **yard or meter** is about . . .
- chair
- arm span

Partitioning

→ dividing shapes into **equal** parts

Halves — 2 equal parts — 1 out of 2 — $\frac{1}{2}$ one half

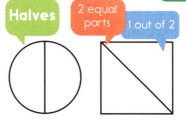

Thirds — 3 equal parts — 1 out of 3 — $\frac{1}{3}$ one third

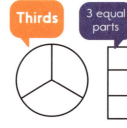

Fourths (or Quarters) — 4 equal parts — 1 out of 4 — $\frac{1}{4}$ one fourth

© Carson Dellosa

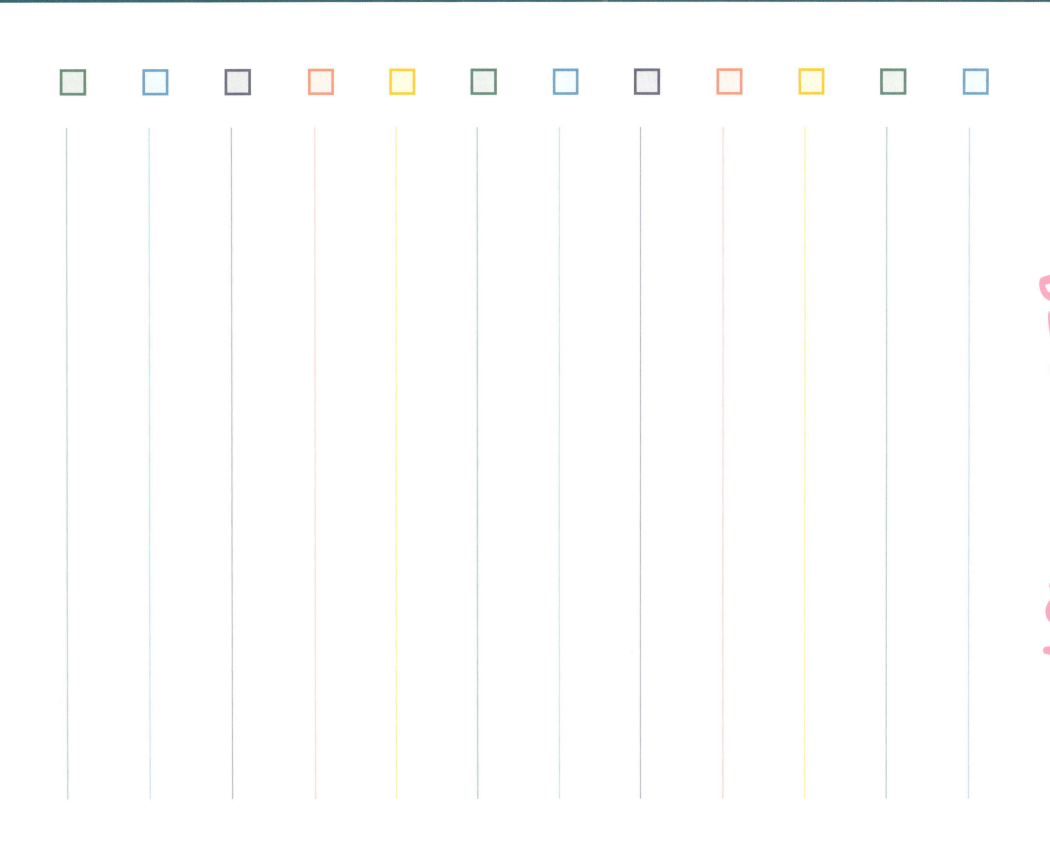